PROVE IT!

HOW TO CREATE A HIGH-PERFORMANCE CULTURE AND MEASURABLE SUCCESS

PROVE IT!

STACEY BARR

WILEY

First published in 2017 by John Wiley & Sons Australia, Ltd
42 McDougall St, Milton Qld 4064

Office also in Melbourne

Typeset in 12.5/14.5 pt Arno Pro

© Stacey Barr Pty Ltd 2017

The moral rights of the author have been asserted

National Library of Australia Cataloguing-in-Publication data:

Creator:	Barr, Stacey, author.
Title:	Prove it!: how to create a high-performance culture and measurable success / Stacey Barr.
ISBN:	9780730336228 (pbk.)
	9780730336242 (ebook)
Notes:	Includes index.
Subjects:	Organizational effectiveness.
	Executive coaching.
	Leadership.
	Performance standards.
	Goal setting in personnel management.
Dewey Number:	658.4

Cover design by Wiley

10 9 8 7 6 5 4 3 2 1

Disclaimer

If you know me, and you know PuMP, then this book is dedicated to YOU. It's because of you that I can keep learning and evolving my ideas on measuring organisational performance. Thank you for giving my work a worthy purpose.

CONTENTS

ABOUT THE AUTHOR

Stacey Barr is a specialist in organisational performance measurement and its application in evidence-based leadership. She has always loved working with numbers, and organisational performance measurement became her niche early in her career.

Since the late 1990s, she has worked with a wide variety of organisations around the world, particularly in the public sector, to help them make their strategy measurable, develop meaningful measures for what matters, and create a performance culture. Stacey believes in evidence, evidence that helps us learn how to make the impact we want, and helps us celebrate the impact we make.

Outside work, her passion is nature and the outdoors, and just about any physical activity that takes her to it: mountain biking, cycling, trail running, kayaking, and hiking.

Her homebase is in semi-rural south-east Queensland, Australia.

ACKNOWLEDGMENTS

Thank you to Ahmed Shoukri, Andrew Garnham, Andrew Phillips, Anneli Karlsson, Anetta Pizag, Becky Thomas, Bryan Dilling, Charles Assey, Chris MacMillan, Claire Janes, Cynthia Abou Khater, Emily Verstege, Emmanuel Aiyenigba, Gerry Prewett, Helen Tilley, Herman Kasro, Jack Spain, Janet Sawatsky, Jennifer Oxtoby, Jesus Garcia, John Morri, Joscelyn Haggarty, Kathleen Simon, Ken McFetridge, Kerrie Donaldson, Lance Jakob, Leanne Ma, Louise Watson, Maryke Savenije, Mike Davidge, Paul Marambos, Peter O'Donnell, Remy Milad, Ruth Hama, Salome Serieys, Scott Maynard, Shahid Hussain Jafri, Todd Pait, Tony Guillen, Ulrike Neumann, Val Purves, and Wayen Miller, who each reviewed the draft of this book and shared additional stories, references and suggestions for style that improved the clarity of the messages I wanted to share. Your encouragement reinforced the need for this book and my confidence in creating it.

Thank you to the team at Wiley — particularly Allison Hiew, Chris Shorten, Clare Dowdell, Ingrid Bond, Lucy Raymond and Theo Vassili — for your helpful, collaborative and professional approach that made each step of bringing this book to fruition so enjoyable. You've all made me a better author.

Finally, thank you to Matt Church for the conversation that inspired the idea and title for this book in the first place.

PREFACE

This is a book for leaders. Organisations have a mission, a vision and a set of strategic goals. They have these things because organisations exist to achieve something, to make some difference in the world, to serve a purpose. And the job of leaders is to bring that to fruition — to make the conceptual goals a tangible reality.

But how can we know how well that's happening, or if it's happening at all? How can we know if we are leading our organisations to make a measurable difference? Most leaders talk about productivity, efficiency, effectiveness, quality, engagement, best practice, sustainability and profitability. And yet we struggle to inspire our leadership team, and everyone throughout the organisation, to:

- do what's most needed to fulfil the mission
- realise the vision
- achieve the strategic goals.

The world is demanding more and more of organisational leaders. The world wants more transparency — to see the truth about how organisations are performing. And not just in terms of profit, but also how they treat people and the planet. The world wants more accountability, holding leaders responsible for the performance of their organisations. Many leaders may be kept awake at night, panicked by what transparency might reveal about their organisation's performance and how they might be held to account.

But the best leaders won't be panicking. The best leaders already know how their organisations are performing, in terms of profit, people and the planet. They know that performance has improved under their leadership, and they can prove it because they measure it. They can prove it because they practise evidence-based leadership.

If we want to know the impact of our leadership on our organisation — if we want to know what legacy we will leave — we have to prove it. And to prove it, we have to measure it. What our gut says, and what 'they' say, is not proof. A finished improvement project or change initiative or capital investment or new product line is not proof. For proof we need objective measures of the results that these investments were supposed to improve.

Measuring performance is like gravity. It pulls our attention and action toward a centre, toward the most important things we should focus on and improve. When we measure the important performance results, we move more directly toward those results and we achieve them sooner and with less effort.

When an eagle circles the sky, hunting for a meal, she sees her prey, she works out how far it is from her, and she lines up the most direct path toward it. Instinctively, she lets gravity pull her toward her goal, effortlessly and rapidly.

For leaders of organisations, performance measurement is the gravity that speeds up and takes effort out of our pursuit of what we want. So we get bigger and better improvements for less effort. And, on an organisational scale, evidence-based leadership is the process of using measurement as the gravity to draw the whole organisation toward the results that matter most.

Evidence-based leaders can prove how well their organisation is delivering what matters most, measurably and objectively and convincingly.

This book is about a system of evidence-based leadership. It maps out the principles, habits and processes that leaders must master to create high-performance organisations. Organisations that can:

- measure their impact
- demonstrate how well they fulfil their mission and realise their vision
- make the world better than they found it.

The evidence-based leadership map is like any map for a territory we want to explore: there isn't only one path to follow. My hope is for this book to guide you through the territory of high-performance organisations. I hope it shows you what's possible, helps you navigate and points out things you otherwise wouldn't have noticed. Let's begin our adventure!

Stacey Barr
September 2016

PART I
WHAT ARE YOU TRYING TO PROVE?

Part I is about the decision to practise evidence-based leadership. It's a choice, after all, so before we explore the framework of evidence-based leadership (in parts II and III), let's take a little time to make an informed decision. We need to be clear about the:

- territory of high-performance organisations
- concept of evidence-based leadership, how it began and where it is going
- price we pay when we practise evidence-based leadership, and the costs we incur when we don't
- framework for how to practise evidence-based leadership.

What's your definition of a high-performance organisation? Let's start by exploring that question.

CHAPTER 1
THE TERRITORY OF HIGH PERFORMANCE

Almost any organisation can prove that it does things. It can prove that it hires people, that those people carry out different tasks, and that money is earned and spent. But what many organisations cannot prove is the most important thing: whether they are fulfilling their purpose or not. High-performance organisations don't just do stuff. They have an impact — ideally, the impact they exist to make. And they can prove how much impact they create.

It starts with purpose

It should be easy to work out the intended impact of any company; it's stated right there in their mission statement. (After all, that's what a mission statement is for.) But that's often not the case! How seriously do you take your organisation's mission and vision, its values and strategic direction? How seriously does your leadership team take them? And your employees? In many organisations, these things exist but are empty platitudes. They exist because they are supposed to exist, and not because they serve any useful purpose. But they should.

The world has evolved far beyond the style of leadership that expected employees to do what they were told and not question managers. People give their best when they work for a cause: something they believe in, that's bigger than themselves and more than their job description. They want a compelling mission and inspiring vision. They want to know that their work is making a difference in the world, and in the future their children will inherit.

Vision and mission statements these days have become pedestrian and clichéd — the thin and empty products of jumping through strategic planning hoops. They've lost the ability to unite masses of people in a shared cause and have imbued more cynicism into workforces. From my experience, the main reason that visions and missions aren't measured is because they are deliberately broad for aspirational purposes, and deliberately vague so everyone can find their own meaning in them. Being broad and vague means being immeasurable.

> People give their best when they work for a cause.

What impact do you think the organisations with the following mission statements intend to make? Can you even tell what types of companies they are, let alone measure their achievement of these goals?

- 'To refresh the world ... To inspire moments of optimism and happiness ... To create value and make a difference.'
- 'To help people and businesses throughout the world realize their full potential.'
- 'Families Making the Difference.'

The first one is The Coca-Cola Company. The second one is Microsoft. The third is PATH, a nonprofit organisation that provides foster care for children with special emotional, behavioural and medical needs. It wasn't obvious, was it? How can such statements be guiding lights to drive the focus, energy and activity of people throughout an organisation when they are this broad and vague? If a strategic direction is not measurable, it's not understandable and it's not recognisable in the world around us.

My purpose here is not to criticise any of these organisations. It might seem unfair to claim that PATH's mission is vague and immeasurable, given that they make such a worthy contribution to the world. If we take that principle to the extreme — that nonprofits don't have to prove their impact — it suggests that if you have a worthy mandate, you don't have to try hard at evidence-based thinking. If nonprofits want to attract more support, and produce the best outcomes possible, they need a clear vision and a measurable impact as much as any organisation.

The importance of clarity

Florence Chadwick was an accomplished open-water swimmer in the 1950s. A legend in her own time, the Californian was the first woman to swim the English Channel in both directions. But when Florence attempted to swim the Catalina Channel a year later, it wasn't the distance and ice-cold water and circling sharks that stopped her. With only a few hundred metres left to swim before she reached her destination of Palos Verde, she gave in. And her reason was fog. She knew that if the fog had cleared and she could see land, she'd have made it. But she couldn't see through the fog and couldn't see that she was making any progress. Only a couple of months later, she tried again. The fog was just as bad, but this time she held a vivid image of her destination firmly in her mind. And she made it. When our vision, our purpose, our direction are specific and clear, they are compelling.

This advice from James Grady, author of *A Simple Statement: A Guide to Non-profit Arts Management and Leadership*, is certainly true of nonprofit organisations, but I believe it's equally true for government and business as well:

> For a non-profit organization, making a profit is not necessarily the definitive measure of success, nor is an increased budget size or staff. The evaluation of success lies in the mission and vision statements and is particular to that organization. Success may represent an increase in audience, in the number of people served by a particular program, or in artistic quality.

The following nonprofit and government organisations' mission statements reflect how clear they are about their purpose. Can you guess the line of work they're in, or even which organisations they are?

- '... creating a community partnership of knowledge, skills and expertise to enrich the participation in life of people who are blind or have low vision and their families. We will ensure that the community recognises their capabilities and contributions.'
- 'To prevent cruelty to animals by actively promoting their care and protection.'
- 'To make Australia the most desirable destination on earth.'
- 'To make Australian sport stronger — to get more people playing sport and to help athletes pursue their dreams.'

The first is from Vision Australia, the second from RSPCA Australia, the third from Tourism Australian, and the last from the Australian Institute of Sport. These are very clear mission statements that make the purpose of the organisation measurable, understandable and recognisable in the world around us.

And what about for-profit companies? Their mission can certainly be more than to make profit. Profit is a by-product of business that is obviously very important to shareholders, but not really important to other stakeholders without whose support the business would simply not exist (customers, the community, employees not rewarded with profit-share). Can you guess which companies (or at least which types of companies) own the following 'beyond profit' mission statements?

- 'To grow a profitable airline ... Where people love to fly ... And where people love to work.'
- 'To care for the world we live in, from the products we make to the ways in which we give back to society. At [company name removed], we strive to set an example for environmental leadership and responsibility — not just in the world of beauty, but around the world.'
- 'To be earth's most customer centric company; to build a place where people can come to find and discover anything they might want to buy online.'

In order, the owners are: Virgin Atlantic, Aveda and Amazon.com. These companies know the power of an inspiring mission, but one that is clear and specific too.

Measuring our vision and mission means choosing a small handful of performance measures that track our progress in making them a reality. They provide real and objective evidence that the organisation is indeed excelling. By measuring the mission of our organisation, whether it's for-profit, nonprofit or government, we take it seriously, we make it tangible and understandable, and we make it easier to align everyone's attention and goals and resources to fulfilling that mission. Our mission is our purpose, and if we don't measure it meaningfully, we can't prove that we're fulfilling that purpose.

Stever Robbins, the Get-It-Done Guy from one of the Quick and Dirty Tips podcasts, says that the ultimate responsibility that rests solely on the CEO's shoulders is the success or failure of the organisation. And the CEO's top two duties, which only they can perform, are building culture and setting strategic direction.

> One of the most important things leaders need to feel is ownership of the organisation's results.

In *What You Really Need to Lead,* Robert Steven Kaplan says leadership starts with an ownership mindset. One of the most important things leaders need to feel is ownership of the organisation's results. That means ownership of the organisation's mission and vision, and ownership of what it takes to make the organisation capable of achieving them.

The high-performance organisation

When we think about high performance in sports, it's easy to understand the term. It's about winning, but it's also about the way the winning is done. Lance Armstrong was everyone's darling in cycling, winning seven Tour de France titles, all of them after battling testicular cancer. But when his use of performance-enhancing drugs throughout his career was uncovered, his titles were stripped and cycling fell out of love with him. Despite his achievements, the deceit and cheating mean he's not a good example of high performance.

The story of Billy Beane and the Oakland A's baseball team is a different matter. Unlike Lance Armstrong, they were performing at the bottom of the league based on wins. But they challenged many of the long-held traditions about how to build a baseball team. They ignored the highest-paid players and recruited players who were rejected or under-used and not valued by more successful teams. Their strategy seemed insane, but the Oakland A's rose to the top rungs of the league on a budget a fraction of the size of their competitors'. They revolutionised the game of baseball. They are a great example of high performance.

In simple terms, a high-performance organisation is one that can perform at a very high level in the game it's playing. The game an organisation is playing is the fulfilment of its mission and the pursuit of its vision. All this means is that a high-performance organisation does well at what it says it wants to do well at.

It's true that there are organisations that say they want to be profitable, and do well at being profitable. There are plenty of organisations that have done this, and at the expense of their people, their customers, or the planet. In their book *How Companies Lie: Why Enron Is Just the Tip of the Iceberg,* authors A. Larry Elliott and Richard J. Schroth discuss how companies like Enron, Tyco and Sunbeam haven't taken care of all their stakeholders: the people that supported them, and whose support they need to last into the future.

> Profit cannot be the ultimate definition of high performance.

Those are not the kinds of organisations that this book was designed for. Profit cannot be the ultimate definition of high performance. It's more than that, and has to be if an organisation is to stand the test of time. And so high performance is more about the culture of an organisation, and the way it pursues results for all its stakeholders. The high-performance culture is one of:

- continuous improvement
- measurement of performance
- alignment with strategy
- consistently reaching for the right targets, without unintended consequences.

Models of excellence

Organisational excellence models such as Baldrige Performance Excellence, the European Foundation for Quality Management (EFQM) and the Australian Business Excellence Framework (ABEF) have been around since the 1990s. These models have been used by many different organisations around the world in their pursuit of high performance. Each model is used in an awards process, where entrants are evaluated by an accredited team against a collection of criteria organised into (usually) seven categories. The seven categories are:

1. *Leadership.* How the organisation's leaders inspire high performance, encourage open communication and transparency, and create a climate for learning, collaboration and success.

2. *Strategic direction and planning.* How the organisation's vision and values and direction are derived, how goals are set at all levels and aligned to the overarching direction, and how people are engaged in executing the strategy.

3. *Data analysis, measurement, information and knowledge.* How the organisation uses data analysis, measurement and reporting of performance and other forms of evidence to inform its decision making, strategy execution and continual improvement of performance.

4. *People and workforce.* How the organisation values its employees and partners, the culture it nurtures, and how it facilitates a safe, healthy and collaborative working environment.

5. *Customer and market focus.* How the organisation understands its customers and their needs, ensures a customer focus throughout the organisation, and positions itself within its market.

6. *Business processes or operations, products and services.* How the organisation has designed the flow of work to develop and deliver its products and services, with an emphasis on systems thinking and cross-functional collaboration, in alignment with strategy.

7. *Results.* How the organisation has defined and attained success, including its impact on customers, its people and society.

Within each of these categories, entrants must demonstrate how they follow some form of quality management plan–do–study–act (PDSA) cycle:

- *Plan.* The organisation has a deliberate approach for the category, such as a framework or process or model.
- *Do.* This approach is deployed or implemented deliberately throughout the organisation.
- *Check.* The results of deploying or implementing the approach are objectively measured.
- *Act.* The measures are used to decide what to continue about the approach and what to modify to get better results.

These organisational excellence models encourage a broader definition of what high performance is. Their philosophy is that high performance is a way of being rather than a place to be. Results, the seventh category, are important, but not at the expense of the other six categories.

In the past, as an evaluator for the Australian Business Excellence Awards, I consistently noticed the weakest link for the majority of organisations was evidence-based thinking. So few could demonstrate, measurably, the results they were creating across each of the seven categories. And, not surprisingly, categories 3 and 7 were always evaluated lower than the others. Seeing this pattern back then, and in every organisation I've worked with since, made me realise we need more evidence-based leaders to inspire and guide their organisations along this journey of high performance.

High performance and the bottom line

We are told that the purpose of business is to make a profit. In the public sector, the parallel is to meet budget. While there are moral reasons why profit ought not be the ultimate purpose of business — for example, when others have to suffer to make those profits possible — there are also sound business reasons why we ought to move away from single measures of success, such as profit. In their book *The Balanced Scorecard*, Robert Steven Kaplan and David P. Norton argue that non-financial performance is just as important as financial performance. This has led to other scorecards, such as the Triple Bottom Line, also aiming for more balance in our definition of success. A scorecard with balance is one where success is defined by the perspectives of every stakeholder affected by a company, and these perspectives give context to what that company measures, monitors and manages. It's not just the financial bottom line that counts.

> High-performance organisations and companies don't solely pursue financial results as their definition of success.

A great example of the consequences of a profit-driven strategy is the factory farming of chickens as described in *The Ethics of What We Eat* by Peter Singer and Jim Mason. To increase profits, some companies maximise the number of birds per square foot of space. (In many operations, chickens get about the size of an A4 sheet of paper to live their lives in.) Aside from the birds' suffering and the stressful work environment for employees, there are some very significant costs to local communities and ecosystems. The ammonia from the chickens' waste makes going outside unbearable for whoever is downwind of the factories and causes irritation and health problems to those exposed. When the waste products are flushed from the factory floor, they run off into nearby streams and waterways and kill the aquatic life. These are the costs that don't make it into the companies' financial statements or annual reports, costs that communities and the environment pay (now and in the future) to subsidise those profits.

High-performance organisations and companies don't solely pursue financial results as their definition of success. They pursue an array of results based on what all their stakeholder groups value most. And they pursue those results in a way that does not depend on other stakeholders paying the costs; how we make the journey to high performance is at least as important as getting there.

So evidence-based leaders start with exceptional:

- clarity about the results that truly do define success for their organisation
- ownership of and responsibility for those results
- care in guiding the organisation to that success.

They give more attention and effort to these three things than most leaders seem to these days. These are the three basic principles of evidence-based leadership.

CHAPTER 2

EVIDENCE-BASED LEADERSHIP

As Pulitzer Prize-winning author Carl Sagan noted in *Cosmos:*

> If we lived on a planet where nothing ever changed, there would be little to do. There would be nothing to figure out. There would be no impetus for science. And if we lived in an unpredictable world, where things changed in random or very complex ways, we would not be able to figure things out. Again, there would be no such thing as science. But we live in an in-between universe, where things change, but according to patterns, rules, or, as we call them, laws of nature...

I find this quote one of the most inspiring motivations for measuring organisational performance. If the world were completely predictable, organisations would be like perfect machines: every outcome would be produced precisely as intended. Control would be at 100 per cent. At this extreme there is no use for measuring performance, because performance is always perfect, with no variation. But our world isn't like that. And that's why performance targets of perfection — such as 'zero injuries' or '100 per cent on-time performance' — feel too confronting for people to commit to, no matter how idealistic or 'right' they might seem. Our organisations are not deterministic machines.

Evidence-based leadership

Conversely, if the world were completely unpredictable, with no order at all, organisations wouldn't exist: the concept of organising would be impossible. Control would be at 0 per cent. At this extreme there would be no use in measuring performance: it would vary so randomly that we could not observe patterns of causation, and would be unable exercise any degree of control over performance. But our world isn't like that either, which is why there is no excuse for decisions to be purely driven by gut feel or hearsay or tradition or whim.

Our world is in between these extremes of perfect predictability and perfect unpredictability. There is variation, but it's not the product of complete randomness. It's the product of complexity, and there is order in this complexity. So in our in-between world we have a use for measuring performance, because it helps us quantify the variation and observe patterns of causation. It helps us learn how we can influence performance by using or changing these patterns.

The purpose of evidence-based leadership is to navigate organisations through a world that is somewhere between the extremes of perfect predictability and perfect unpredictability, and measurement is the primary tool of the evidence-based leader. Performance measurement deepens our understanding of the complexity in our organisations, and speeds up our identification of patterns, so we can constantly improve at creating the results we want.

> Measurement is the primary tool of the evidence-based leader.

Evidence-based leadership is not a mainstream practice in business. According to authors Jeffrey Pfeffer and Robert I. Sutton in their book *Hard Facts, Dangerous Half-Truths and Total Nonsense*:

> Business decisions, as many of our colleagues in business and your own experience can attest, are frequently based on hope or fear, what others seem to be doing, what senior leaders have done and believe has worked in the past, and their dearly held ideologies—in short, on lots of things other than the facts…If doctors practiced medicine the way many companies practice management, there would be far more sick and dead patients, and many more doctors would be in jail.

The rise of evidence-based management

The *Harvard Business Review* began publishing articles on evidence-based management in the mid 2000s, largely triggered by Pfeffer and Sutton's book, which describes evidence-based management as follows:

> Evidence-based management proceeds from the premise that using better, deeper logic and employing facts to the extent possible permits leaders to do their jobs better. Evidence-based management is based on the belief that facing the hard facts about what works and what doesn't, understanding the dangerous half-truths that constitute so much conventional wisdom about management, and rejecting the total nonsense that too often passes for sound advice will help organizations perform better.

The Center for Evidence-Based Management (CEBMa) takes this definition of evidence-based management further, by outlining a process for practising it:

> Evidence-based practice is about making decisions through conscientious, explicit and judicious use of the best available evidence from multiple sources …

We practise evidence-based management to increase the likelihood of achieving the results we want from the organisation we're managing.

Evidence-based leadership is the application of evidence-based management at the most strategic level in an organisation. It has to be practised and prioritised by all of the senior leadership team, including the CEO and board members. If it isn't, then evidence-based management at lower levels won't happen quickly or comprehensively enough for an organisation to fulfil its mission and reach its vision.

Leaders hold the space for high performance

Evidence-based leadership is more than evidence-based management. An organisation's leaders must not only practise evidence-based management to elevate organisational performance at the strategic level — they must also inspire and encourage and expect it from everyone else in the organisation.

When we are practising evidence-based management, we are using objective evidence to design and monitor the organisation's strategy. This evidence primarily comes from performance measures that monitor our progress toward the vision, mission and strategic goals. Other forms of evidence, such as research and case studies and experimental results, inform us of the best ways to make that progress happen sooner, or in larger steps, or with higher returns on our investment.

When we are inspiring and encouraging and expecting evidence-based management from everyone in the organisation, we are making it easier for them to practise it themselves and apply it to what matters most. We need to:

- make it part of our routine language and everyday conversations
- coach others in how to practise it and how to align their decisions with what is strategically important
- recognise and reward the learning and practice of evidence-based management even more than its impact
- support the practice of evidence-based management by providing:
  — how-to processes
  — a clear and measurable strategy
  — evidence-based reporting frameworks
  — analytical tools
  — conversation outlines
  — in-person participation.

Leaders are responsible for the direction and the culture of an organisation, and the culture of high performance will come only when they both practise and inspire evidence-based management. This is what I mean by 'holding the space' for high performance. So we might define evidence-based leadership as the following two approaches:

1. The application of evidence-based management at the whole-organisation level and the active and routine support of its application organisation-wide.
2. The alignment of all decision making and action with the purpose and strategic direction of the organisation.

These two approaches will measurably elevate the overall performance of the organisation and its positive impact in the world.

Managers and supervisors and staff will not practise evidence-based management without it being deliberately led from the top. What the CEO talks about and does, the rest of the organisation talks about and does. Evidence-based leaders routinely talk about:

- the purpose of the organisation
- the evidence that the purpose is being fulfilled
- what that evidence says about how well that's happening.

There are no short cuts. If we want high-performance organisations, we have to be evidence-based leaders, every single day.

CHAPTER 3

KNOWING IS A DOUBLE-EDGED SWORD

The most visible leader in almost any country is that country's political leader. In Australia, Prime Minister Malcolm Turnbull was interviewed by Leigh Sales on *7.30* following his re-election. She was attempting to nail down some of the results that the government would achieve over the upcoming term. When Sales asked how the public should judge the government's performance, Turnbull replied:

> Well the public should judge us against the delivery of the commitments that we have made…[The government's performance] will be measured against many different criteria, but the fundamental measurement, of course, is 'are the projects underway', 'are they being delivered', 'are they being delivered on-budget'.

This is a rather typical response from many political leaders about how they define success: that promises (which often means projects) will be implemented.

But the results we want from our government aren't that it invests taxpayers' money on projects. It's that our way of life is improved thanks to these projects. But to measure how much better specific aspects of our lives actually become is risky in a political environment. Anything less than a perfect result is attacked by the Opposition and by vocal community groups, and these attacks slow down and sabotage progress. The broad, complex and intangible results that make up a better way of life are never completely within the control of any one person or group or political party, and so perfect results are impossible. What is far more controllable, and therefore less subject to attack, is the action a group or person takes. But it's far less useful, because we don't learn whether these actions are working or not, and how we can improve the return on investment in them.

Evidence cuts both ways

Being an evidence-based leader is a double-edged sword. Evidence becomes both a tool in our hand and a rod for our back. It is how we learn about the true performance of our organisation, so we can manage it and also manage how we are judged for that performance. We cannot have the former without the latter.

> Evidence becomes both a tool in our hand and a rod for our back.

So the price for informed decision making is transparency and accountability. And that's a price that appears too high for many leaders. They keep their heads in the sand and steer by gut feel; they distract with hearsay and anecdote and biased selection of data. But what these leaders don't realise is that the price of transparency and accountability is much lower than the price of ignorance. Organisations led by such leaders rarely perform well. And if they perform well in something, it's usually short-lived and at the expense of other important results.

Authors Jeffrey Pfeffer and Robert Sutton say it this way:

> The implication is that leaders need to make a fundamental decision: do they want to be told they are always right, or do they want to lead organizations that actually perform well?

In truth, most of us would like it both ways: to always be right and to have an organisation that is performing well. But we need to decide what's more important.

Managers and employees understand the tension of making Pfeffer and Sutton's decision. One of my regular blog readers, Jesus, shared with me a story that illustrates this point precisely. A politician in Jesus's homeland of Spain wanted a regular detailed report about how procurement of goods and services was performing. The politician met with the procurement manager, a very experienced public servant, who agreed to produce the report. As the procurement manager headed out the door, he turned to the politician and asked him, 'Are you sure you want to get this report? I mean, if you get this information, you will be forced to take action.' The procurement manager was asking the politician to make Pfeffer and Sutton's decision: did he want the report to tell him that procurement was performing well, or did he want the report to tell him how it was actually performing?

Transparency, accountability, impotence

One of my earliest teachers in organisational performance was the safety manager in a transport organisation. He invited me to help him improve safety performance reporting, and part of my improvement was to display the safety performance measures in line charts with about two years of history. This was so we could see how performance changed over time, track the impact of our improvement initiatives and see the potential for further improvement.

This was what I assumed the safety manager was indeed trying to do. But I was wrong. He wanted to know that what he was doing was working. Not *if*, but *that* it was working. The improved graphs I showed him told a different story: they showed that nothing had changed over the past two years. Performance was not improving under his leadership.

Without realising it, the safety manager had taken Pfeffer and Sutton's first option in their fundamental decision: to be told he was always right. And the price he paid was impotence: the lack of any effect at all on safety performance. And, of course, that was the price his organisation also had to pay.

In contrast, Jon, the CEO of a timber products company and one of my favourite clients, took Pfeffer and Sutton's second decision: to lead his organisation to actually perform well. He was frustrated that he couldn't see any bottom-line impact from all the investments the company was making in improving processes. Rather than hiding this from his board, making excuses or looking for data that would paint a positive picture, Jon took ownership of the reality.

He and his senior leadership team spent the time to learn how to measure the company's strategic direction, over and above profit. They aligned each operational team with that strategic direction and helped them learn how to measure the operational results that were drivers of the strategic results. They used the measures as a cornerstone in their evidence-based management. And it became easier to align their process improvement projects to the strategic results, and the bottom line.

Transparency and accountability are demanded of organisations now, and they are required in order to truly know how an organisation is performing. And, of course, accountability means that the organisation's leaders will take responsibility for actual performance if it's below expectation.

Our world needs more courageous leaders who will accept the price of transparency and accountability and pursue high performance. Because that's really the only way that things get better.

Which decision have you made?

CHAPTER 4

HOW TO BECOME AN EVIDENCE-BASED LEADER

Evidence-based leadership is not about how to lead. It's about what to give our attention to as we lead. It's not about how to communicate or how to inspire or how to direct or how to engage. It's about how to apply all these attributes to create a high-performance organisation.

What we give our attention to as we lead is the performance of the organisation. We communicate the results that matter, so everyone understands them. We inspire everyone to reach for higher performance targets, to achieve the results that matter. We set direction and help each team find their contribution to it. We engage everyone so they feel ownership of their contribution. How we lead is important, and what we emphasise through our leadership is just as important.

> Evidence-based leadership is not about how to lead. It's about what to give our attention to as we lead.

To lead an organisation to high performance, a strong emphasis must be given to the role of evidence. Evidence-based leaders pursue high performance by speeding up the cycle of closing performance gaps — the gaps between where the organisation's performance is right now, and where they want it to be. This is why evidence-based leaders give a lot of attention to results-based performance measures.

The foundation of high performance is measurement

All leaders are responsible for how their organisation performs. This is assessed by the results the organisation achieves, not by the work it performs. To truly know how an organisation is performing, and whether it's getting better over time, those results must be measured.

> Without good performance measures, we have no evidence. With no evidence, we can't know.

Performance measures are evidence of the degree to which important results are occurring over time. Without good performance measures, we have no evidence. With no evidence, we can't know.

Evidence-based leaders give their attention to:

- the results that matter most, so they can fulfil the organisation's mission and realise its vision
- objective and relevant measures that tell them how those results are tracking, so they can know the next performance gaps to close
- the alignment of their organisation's policies, processes and systems to produce the results that matter most, so their finite resources are leveraged to get the biggest performance improvements.

Leaders give attention to these factors as they:

- set the direction for the organisation
- monitor its progress
- decide what change initiatives to invest in.

And giving attention to these factors is not just for leaders; it's for everyone in the organisation. Everyone has to:

- work in ways that help achieve the corporate direction set by the leaders
- show up to work each day and know that they are contributing to something bigger than their to-do list
- get involved in tweaking and transforming the organisation so it can better fulfil its mission and realise its vision.

So evidence-based leaders also give their attention to the way this is carried out throughout their entire organisation.

The habits of evidence-based leadership

There are three leadership habits of high performance that evidence-based leaders master. They personally practise them, and by practising them routinely they become role models for their organisations. These leadership habits are called *Direction*, *Evidence* and *Execution*, as shown in figure 4.1.

Figure 4.1: the three leadership habits of evidence-based leadership

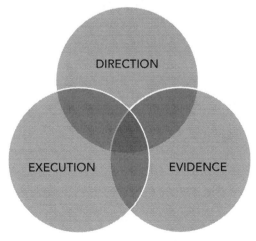

Direction is about articulating a well-designed strategy that is results-oriented, understandable to everyone, and ruthlessly prioritised.

Evidence is about setting meaningful performance measures for each strategic goal that are quantitative, aligned to what matters and focused on improvement. *Execution* is about implementing the corporate strategy and achieving the strategic goals using the leverage found in the continuous improvement of business processes.

Through the practice, and ultimately the mastery, of these leadership habits, leaders inspire high-performance habits organisation-wide. These organisational habits are *Decision*, *Action* and *Learning*, as shown in figure 4.2.

Figure 4.2: the organisational habits that evidence-based leaders inspire

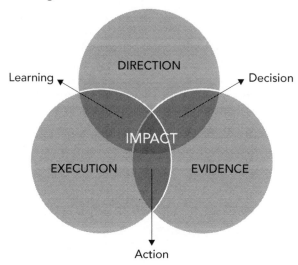

Decision is about helping people take ownership of the results that matter by role-modelling ownership, getting their buy-in and giving them a clear line of sight to the corporate strategy. *Action* is about helping people get the right things done to achieve the results that matter, through a focus on causal analysis, practicality and collaboration. *Learning* is about helping people work *on* the business as a normal part of their work, by adopting an experimental mindset, learning from failure and iterating to success.

The leadership habits are practised by evidence-based leaders in their own domain of corporate strategy. And the organisational habits are what evidence-based leaders will inspire throughout the organisation, from top to bottom. If an organisation is already achieving high performance, these habits are already ingrained as part of the cultural norms and business-as-usual practices. If an organisation has not yet mastered these habits, it's likely that some mindsets are getting in the way.

The mindsets of evidence-based leadership

A mindset is a collection of attitudes toward something. Often our attitudes get in the way of how we see things, such as new choices or better practices. Over the two decades I've worked in the organisational performance space, I have seen a common set of mindsets that stop leaders from seeing new choices and practices for getting their organisations to perform. Figure 4.3 shows the most important mindset shifts that need to be made to pursue high performance.

Figure 4.3: the mindsets of evidence-based leadership

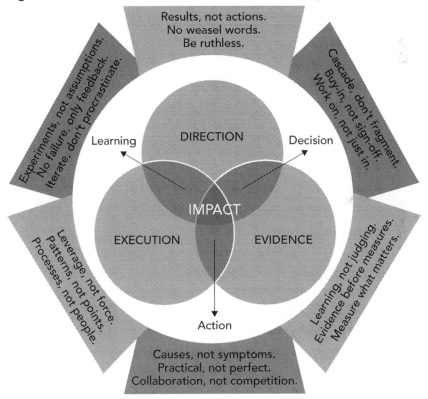

Mindsets for *Direction*

For the leadership habit of *Direction*, the following three mindsets help us articulate a well-designed strategy that is results-oriented, understandable to everyone and ruthlessly prioritised:

1. *Results, not actions.* Write strategic goals that are results-oriented, not action-oriented (action comes later).

2. *No weasel words.* Clearly articulate the strategic goals in language everyone will understand (they can't buy into what they don't understand).

3. *Be ruthless.* Ruthlessly prioritise the strategic goals to focus on performance results that matter most, right now (the more goals you have, the fewer you'll achieve).

Mindsets for *Evidence*

For the leadership habit of *Evidence*, the following three mindsets help us set meaningful performance measures for each strategic goal that are quantitative, aligned to what matters and focused on improvement:

1. *Learning, not judging.* Use evidence to learn like a scientist learns, without judgement.

2. *Evidence before measures.* Design measures as quantifications of the observable results.

3. *Measure what matters.* Only measure what can be aligned to the priorities: mission, vision and strategic goals.

Mindsets for *Execution*

For the leadership habit of *Execution*, the following three mindsets help us implement the corporate strategy and achieve the strategic goals, using the leverage found in continuous improvement of business processes:

1. *Leverage, not force.* Implement or execute strategy based on working smarter, not harder.

2. *Patterns, not points.* Make strategy execution about removing and managing variability, not about hitting the numbers.

3. *Processes, not people.* Execute strategy to improve business processes and how work is designed, not to control people and what work is done.

Mindsets for *Decision*

To inspire the organisational habit of *Decision*, the following three mindsets help us guide people to take ownership of the results that matter by role-modelling ownership, getting their buy-in and giving them a clear line of sight to the corporate strategy:

1. *Cascade, don't fragment.* Create a line of sight from every team to the corporate direction and delegate the authority to improve.
2. *Buy-in, not sign-off.* Communicate the corporate direction in a way that engages everyone.
3. *Work on, not just in.* Give the authority (priority, time and resources) to work *on* the business and not just in it.

Mindsets for *Action*

To inspire the organisational habit of *Action*, the following three mindsets help us guide people to achieve the results that matter through a focus on causal analysis, practicality and collaboration:

1. *Causes, not symptoms.* Find ways to remove the constraints that limit capability rather than compensating for lack of capability.
2. *Practical, not perfect.* Build the momentum of performance improvement by progressing when it's 80 per cent perfect, rather than waiting for 100 per cent.
3. *Collaboration, not competition.* Find and fix the problems that exist in the white space on the organisational chart: the handover points between business units, functions and teams.

Mindsets for *Learning*

To inspire the organisational habit of *Learning*, the following three mindsets help us guide people to work *on* the business as a normal part of their work by adopting an experimental mindset, learning from failure and iterating to success:

1. *Experiments, not assumptions.* Never stop learning and discovering and re-understanding.
2. *No failure, only feedback.* Celebrate learning — whether it comes from success or failure.
3. *Iterate, don't procrastinate.* Set shorter time frames and smaller goals to build the muscle of high performance.

Let's unpack these habits and mindsets, so you can start practising the pieces of evidence-based leadership that you would like to master.

PART I
IN SUMMARY

High-performance organisations excel at creating the impact they were designed to create, for all their stakeholders. High-performance organisations value more than just the bottom line. They value the fulfilment of their mission and the realisation of their vision. And they can prove how well they're performing in both.

High-performance organisations are led by evidence-based leaders. But evidence-based leadership is not about *how* to lead. We already do that. It's about *what* to give our attention to as we lead, if a high-performance organisation is truly our goal. One of the fundamental things evidence-based leaders give their attention to is results-based performance measures — the information that tells them what they really need to know to create and maintain high performance. They prefer to pay the price of transparency and accountability, rather than incur the cost of ignorance.

Evidence-based leadership is more than evidence-based management, or making decisions from fact rather than gut feel or hearsay or opinion. It's about holding the space for the whole organisation to practise the behaviours of high performance, leading by example.

Evidence-based leaders practise three leadership habits: *Direction*, *Evidence* and *Execution*. And they inspire in everyone else the three organisational habits of *Decision*, *Action* and *Learning*.

In Part II, we dive deep into the three habits of *Direction*, *Evidence* and *Execution* and how to master them.

PART II
HABITS OF EVIDENCE-BASED LEADERSHIP

There are three leadership habits that the evidence-based leader masters. These habits are about our own personal practices: the kind of role model we are for our organisation. These habits are called *Direction, Evidence* and *Execution*:

- *Direction* is about articulating a well-designed strategy that is:
    — results-oriented
    — understandable to everyone
    — ruthlessly prioritised.
- *Evidence* is about setting meaningful performance measures for each strategic goal that are:
    — focused on improvement
    — quantitative
    — aligned to what matters.
- *Execution* is about implementing the corporate strategy and achieving the strategic goals through change initiatives that are focused on:
    — leverage and return on investment
    — reducing variability
    — improving processes.

As leaders, it's our responsibility to set the direction for the organisation, to measure its achievement, and to execute the change initiatives that will achieve it. It's our responsibility, but many leaders have limiting mindsets about how they do these things. As a result, the organisation's direction is vague and un-compelling, no-one knows how much of it is truly achieved, and too much time and money is wasted on change initiatives that don't work. Evidence-based leaders have different mindsets. And now we'll explore what they are.

CHAPTER 5

DIRECTION: MAKE IT UNDERSTOOD AND IT WILL BE MEASURABLE

Leading an organisation is much more complex than navigating a ship across vast oceans. There are many more variables and forces interplaying, and we don't yet have the instruments and charts to detect or predict them all. But the fundamental principle of direction is the same: if the captain isn't clear about where to go and how to hold course when the seas get rough and the crew gets worried and confused, the voyage fails. Leaders of organisations need to be clear about the destination, and how to hold course when the pressure is on. This is the habit of articulating a clear direction.

Direction means strategy

A clear direction is not about business as usual. It's about strategy, and strategy is about:

- change
- improvement
- working *on* the business and not *in* it.

There is a difference between a business plan and a business model. The business model is how we've designed our systems and processes and structures to create the results our organisation exists to deliver. But the business strategy is about how to change and improve that business model — to better deliver the same results, or get new results.

An organisation's strategic direction describes:

- the results that define the success of the organisation as a whole
- its impact in the world
- the results that currently have the most leverage to improve the whole-of-organisation results.

A good strategic direction is where evidence-based leadership begins. And a good strategic direction that can support evidence-based leadership will be much easier when we have these three specific mindsets:

1. *Results, not actions.* Write strategic goals that are results-oriented, not action-oriented (action comes later).
2. *No weasel words.* Clearly articulate the strategic goals in language everyone will understand (they can't buy into what they don't understand).
3. *Be ruthless.* Ruthlessly prioritise the strategic goals to focus on performance results that matter most, right now (the more goals you have, the fewer you'll achieve).

These qualities aren't commonly evident in most strategy. Their absence is one of the reasons leaders find it so hard to practise evidence-based leadership, and why they feel so uncomfortable with transparency and accountability.

Let's start with the first of these mindsets: a good strategic direction is results-based, not action-oriented.

Results, not actions

Results describe states or qualities that are enduring. *Actions* describe the carrying out of a task or project that should create or improve a specific result.

Evidence-based leadership makes no sense if there are no results to strive for. If the strategic direction is a simply a list of initiatives or projects or things to get done, then people confuse success with completion. But there is little point in getting stuff done if we're not aiming that effort at the results we want to achieve. For example, there's no point in completing an initiative to set up a customer relationship management system unless everyone is clear that the result is to retain profitable customers. When we know the results we want to achieve, evidence-based leadership has a context.

> When we know the results we want to achieve, evidence-based leadership has a context.

But too often strategy is written as a list of initiatives or projects or things to get done, and there is no result in sight.

- *From a local council:* The region is promoted as a welcoming place to live and grow.
- *From a transport department:* Build a network of priority bus corridors.
- *From a procurement team:* Communicate with customers.

If we take each of these initiatives and ask why we're bothering to do them, we'll get a good start at figuring out what the results are. Why would a local council want to promote the region? When I asked them, they said they wanted two results:

1. The region attracts new residents.
2. The region retains its residents.

Why would a transport department want to build a network of priority bus corridors? It could be any one of the following results:

- Commuters get to and from work quickly.
- Traffic flows faster during peak hours.
- People choose public transport instead of driving.

Why would a procurement team want to communicate with customers? Which customers, and communicate with them about what? To achieve what result? It turns out that the result they wanted was this: 'Internal customers follow the purchasing policy.'

Aligning projects with results

It isn't an either/or decision to be project-oriented or results-oriented. We need to be both, but at the right time. We need to be project-oriented when we are managing the activities and initiatives we've invested in. And we need to be results-oriented to make sure we choose the right activities and initiatives, and that those investments aren't a waste of time, effort and money. That's why the evidence-based leadership habit of *Direction* comes before *Execution*.

This is the difference between program management and performance management. Program management monitors milestones and expenditure to keep projects on track. Performance management monitors performance measures to keep the results on track. Both are part of evidence-based leadership, but the former is only ever going to add value when the latter is defined clearly first. When people are only project-oriented, waste is guaranteed.

> When people are only project-oriented, waste is guaranteed.

Performance does not equate to completing projects on time and on budget. The only reason we invest time and money into projects is to make a needed difference, or have a specific impact, or achieve a particular result. If we don't know what the objective is then how can we know that we've chosen the right project? How can we know if we've designed the project in the right way, and implemented it well? If we don't know, then we're guessing. And acting on guesses will always cause many times more waste than acting on knowledge.

Of course, not much will change if people are only results-oriented. Being clear about the results we're striving to achieve is motivating and focusing. We get everyone's energy aligned toward the same end goal. Collaboration is easier, and so is decision making when problems or difficult choices arise. But without action, results never become reality. We sit around theorising and visioning and never get anything done. This breeds cynicism and apathy.

Marrying results-oriented and project-oriented thinking

We need to marry results-oriented and project-oriented thinking, not choose one over the other, and not mistake one for the other. We're not focusing on results instead of projects. We're putting results and projects in the right order. That way, the projects can be celebrated when they successfully get the results that they were intended to create.

A simple conversation can help expand the mindsets of project-oriented people, so they can appreciate their projects in a results context. For example, we could start simply, by discussing just one project. In local government, a typical project is to create and deliver a new community program, such as promoting sporting clubs. Then we could ask them what change in the community this project will make if (or when) it succeeds. They might say it's to increase community participation in organised community activities. That's the result.

Then we could ask them how they would recognise that result in the real world. They might say that they'd see club memberships growing, and more people using sporting venues in the community. That's the start of finding the right measures. The value of being clear about the results and the measures is that it's far more exciting to celebrate success, and it ensures we are getting the biggest bang for our buck. People don't pay rates and taxes to be educated on the benefits of sporting clubs — they pay for a happy and healthy lifestyle in their community.

Finally, we could ask them how they feel now that they've linked the project to a valuable result. We could ask them if they'd feel excited knowing this result was achieved because of their project. This kind of conversation will plant the seed of results-oriented thinking that gives project-oriented thinking a reason. It's a small step, but small steps are easier to start and easier to nurture. And when we, as leaders, write the corporate strategy in a results-oriented way, it provides a great example for others in creating results-oriented goals.

All meaningful strategic directions are results-oriented first, before initiatives are designed and chosen. But there is still another common struggle with how strategic direction is written, even when it is results-oriented. That brings us to the second important mindset of the leadership habit of *Direction*: clearly articulating the strategic goals in language everyone will understand.

> All meaningful strategic directions are results-oriented first.

RESULTS, NOT ACTIONS

Evidence-based leadership makes no sense if there are no results to strive for. If the strategic direction is a simply a list of initiatives or projects or things to get done, then people confuse success with completion.

No weasel words

One of the worst problems with strategy is the excessive use of 'weasely' language. And you'll know what I mean if your strategy is full of words such as 'efficiency', 'capacity', 'diversity', 'quality', 'fit for purpose', 'holistic', 'productivity', 'sustainability', or 'outcomes'.

Wikipedia, which is in a constant battle to scrub weasel words from its entries, explains the concept:

> A weasel word, or anonymous authority, is an informal term for words and phrases aimed at creating an impression that a specific or meaningful statement has been made, when instead only a vague or ambiguous claim has actually been communicated.

Don Watson was an Australian political speech–writer and is author of many books, and he has also taken a stand on weasel words. Particularly interesting is what he has to say in his book *Death Sentence: The Decay of Public Language*:

> There have been signs of decay in the language of politics and academia for years, but the direst symptoms are in business; and the curse has spread

through the pursuit of business models in places that were never businesses...The public sector spouts it as loudly as the private does. It is the language of all levels of government including the very local. They speak of focusing on the delivery of outputs and matching decisions to strategic initiatives. Almost invariably these strategic initiatives are key strategic initiatives...It is the grey death of the globalised world.

Look at these strategic goals:

- 'A strong and effective network and corporate function which works collaboratively with partners to build capability, support delivery and enhance accountability to ensure the positive reputation of the Department.' (Department of Employment, Australia.)
- 'Increased national capacity to ensure availability of and access to services and to strengthen systems.' (UNICEF.)
- 'Libraries ensure effective, efficient and responsible stewardship of resources.' (Hamilton City Libraries.)

These empty and inert words sound important but fail to say to anything at all. The problems with weasel words outweigh any reason we might offer for using them.

There's no good reason to keep weasel words

There are five common reasons why we use weasel words to articulate and communicate our strategic direction:

1. *To make alignment easier.* We believe it's important to keep the goals broad enough for everyone to find their own contribution to them. But that's a myth. People find it frustrating, and they turn off and can even become cynical about the strategy when it's written so vaguely. This is why many strategic plans just sit on the shelf, gathering dust. It's why people talk about it but you don't see it manifested in their activities.

2. *Our strategy is complex.* We believe our strategy is very sophisticated and we need sophisticated words to convey

it. But while we might think we have a good handle on the practical meaning of those big words that articulate our goals, we have to remember that a strategic plan isn't written for us. It's written for everyone else. It's the rest of the organisation's efforts that will execute that strategy. If they don't understand it, it won't be executed.

3. *To avoid wasting time in debate.* We believe it is impossible to replace those weasel words with much more specific words we can all agree on. But if we can't agree on the words to replace the weasel words, it likely means we don't have a shared understanding of their intent in the first place. Big problem! It means that the best conversation we can have is definitely the conversation about what those weasel words mean to each of us, and how to agree on what they should mean.

4. *Being specific locks us in.* We don't want to be locked into achieving anything too specific; we prefer to have room to move. This is a fear of failure. And that fear is the thing to address first, before the weasel words. If it's a fear of missing targets, we're driving the wrong behaviour. The behaviour we want is to take action that moves performance closer to targets. And that can only happen when everyone is clear about what action is needed, when it's needed, and why.

5. *We'd have too many goals.* We realise that if we made each weasel word specific, it could mean several important things. It's true: often when a goal is de-weaselled, it turns into half-a-dozen specific results. That's too many. It's a sign that our strategy isn't really strategic. It's more like a shopping list of everything that is important, rather than a ruthless prioritisation of what is most important and urgent to focus on right now. One of management guru Peter Drucker's most important messages is this: strategy is more about what *not* to do.

None of these five reasons is strong enough to excuse us for writing strategic goals in 'management speak' or 'weasel words'. With a vague articulation of the organisation's purpose and priorities, we can't ever know if they are being achieved. And that means we don't know exactly what we are leading our organisation to.

What to replace weasel words with

Take a highlighter to your strategic plan and tag any word that a 10-year-old would not understand. Where we have used weasel words, we must define specifically what we mean by them or accept the fact that we'll forever struggle to find meaningful ways to know whether or not our goals are happening, and our strategy will remain open for interpretation. Ambiguity is definitely not a recipe for high performance; it's a recipe for confusion. Incidentally, did you know that a collective of weasels is called a confusion? It's also known as a 'sneak' of weasels!

> Ambiguity is definitely not a recipe for high performance; it's a recipe for confusion.

The easiest way to change a weasel word to something more meaningful and specific is to try and explain it to a 10-year-old. This does not mean 'dumbing down' our goal; it means making it easy to understand, for everyone. For example, in the goal 'Enhance our protection of our landscape', almost every word is weasely. It's too broad to measure, and it's too vague to be sure that everyone will share the same understanding of it. A local council in New South Wales avoided weasel words and wrote this goal in 10-year-old language: 'The fragile soils of ridges and escarpments and valuable farming land are protected from unnatural erosion and loss of topsoil.'

Straight away we can visualise what this goal means. We see in our mind's eye rolling hills and rocky outcrops, the earthy patchwork of crops, vast green pastures with cows or sheep grazing. We see black or red topsoil in some places, and grey and cracked earth in other places. We see what we can measure: the amount of erosion and the amount of topsoil.

In addition to being nearly impossible to measure meaningfully, and hardly ever comprehensible to everyone in the organisation, weasel words also hide another problem: a strategy that is too broad and unfocused. The third important mindset of the leadership habit of *Direction* deals with this directly: ruthlessly prioritising the strategic goals to focus on the performance results that matter most, right now.

Be ruthless

Peter Drucker is quoted over and again for his message that the key to strategy is omission. Good strategy is more about what *not* to do than it is about what to do. And that's the product of ruthless prioritisation.

In *The 4 Disciplines of Execution*, authors Sean Covey, Chris McChesney and Jim Huling suggest the first discipline is to focus on the wildly important. Achieving goals for change amidst the whirlwind of day-to-day work follows the law of diminishing returns. If we have two or three goals over and above the whirlwind, we can achieve those two or three goals. But if we have four to 10 goals, in addition to our whirlwind, we'll achieve only one or two of them. You know how many goals can be achieved when we have 11 or more goals to achieve, as well as our whirlwind? That's right: none.

Should, can, will

We cannot afford to have too many goals in our strategy. We have to be ruthless to create high performance. And to be ruthless, we must only keep goals that can pass the 'should, can, will' test.

Before we even consider measuring a goal, we ask three questions of it:

1. *Should* the goal be pursued? (Is it important enough, right now?)
2. *Can* we pursue it? (Is it inside our circle of influence?)
3. *Will* we pursue it? (Do we have the time and resources to improve it?)

If we answer yes to all three questions, the goal is measure-worthy. If it's not measure-worthy, then why is it in the strategy? Why are we aiming to achieve something but not interested in knowing

We must only keep goals that can pass the 'should, can, will' test.

whether it's achieved or not? It doesn't make sense.

Simplify by visualising

Bec was a performance analysis and reporting consultant with a state's department of education. I first met Bec when she attended one of my PuMP Blueprint Workshops to learn how to make measuring performance easier and more meaningful. When she returned to work after the training, she used PuMP (see p.49 for more details on this) to help one of the state's country schools to develop more meaningful performance measures. She started by helping them to visually map out all their performance results and how they related to one another. This school had fairly high levels of disadvantage, and a review recommended specific improvements needed in their performance. As a result, the school's leadership team wanted to update their three-year improvement plan and invited Bec to help with their targets.

It turned out that they wanted to improve everything. Looking at their improvement plan, they had five priorities. But within each of those priorities there were four or five goals. When Bec helped them to map the specific performance results implied by all their goals, it became clear that for their literacy priority alone there were 115 goals to achieve in three years.

Their plan had never been presented visually before, and that was the biggest impact of the results map for this leadership team. It made it clear they were trying to improve too much. With 115 goals, it's impossible to thoroughly do that improvement work. The results map also helped them to see duplication and unnecessary overlap in their goals. It helped them distinguish the most important improvements from the myriad things that were business as usual.

They ended up with four goals for the school as a whole, and just a few measures for those goals. They were ruthless; they focused on the wildly important to increase the probability that the wildly important would be achieved with excellence.

Leaders who take on too much and set many lofty goals should not be held up as the heroes. They won't achieve those goals and, if they do, the price will be too high. It's the leaders who focus like a laser beam — and achieve big improvements that can sustain themselves beyond the effort — that are the real heroes. It's these leaders who change the world.

BE RUTHLESS

We have to be ruthless to create high performance. And to be ruthless, we must only keep goals that can pass the 'should, can, will' test.

When our strategy is results-oriented, easy to understand and focused, it becomes measurable. And measures are a cornerstone of evidence-based leadership. And a measurable strategy should be measured! Naturally then, the next leadership habit is *Evidence*.

CHAPTER 6

EVIDENCE: ANYTHING THAT MATTERS CAN BE MEASURED

What is more urgent than measuring the results that matter most to us? The way most organisations function, you'd think that just about everything else is more urgent than measuring. Sure, people say that measuring the results that matter is *important*, but it does tend to fall to the bottom of everyone's to-do list.

Evidence means measuring

If you were to ask me, I'd say that *nothing* is more urgent than measuring what matters. Most of those other things that are higher on the to-do list include fixing problems, reacting to other people's priorities and catching up on overdue milestones. These so-called urgent things are actually the product of *not* measuring what matters!

If we don't measure the results that matter, then we really have little idea if we're achieving them. Unless we are measuring what matters, and measuring it well, we can be certain that:

- we're delaying the achievement of our goals
- we're not investing in the highest-leverage change initiatives
- our 'urgent' basket will always be overflowing.

Without measures, luck plays a bigger role than it should in our desired results becoming reality.

Scorecards aren't measures

One of the first mistakes people make in their pursuit of measures is to assume the strategic planning model they use to design their strategic goals and change initiatives will produce them. When I started my career in performance measurement, *The Balanced Scorecard* was first published. It was heralded as the best way to measure organisational performance that had ever been developed. And it's true to say *The Balanced Scorecard* has been a revolution in organisational performance measurement. The revolution was the idea of a scorecard of measures, both financial and non-financial, that align to strategy and link together to tell the story of what is strategically important. But *The Balanced Scorecard* does not provide a method for designing measures of performance.

There is nothing at all in *The Balanced Scorecard* that guides us on how exactly to design performance measures for strategic objectives. Sure, it explains why we need a scorecard of measures that is balanced, and how to get that balance. But there is nothing about how exactly to decide what the measures themselves should be, and how to implement them, and how to report and interpret and use them to drive performance improvement.

The practical, on-the-ground struggles that I (and every executive and strategy professional I've met in my 20-year performance measurement career) had were not addressed at all by *The Balanced*

Scorecard. That's because it's more a strategy design approach than it is a performance measurement method. The same can be said for many other so-called measurement methods and frameworks: Program Logic Model, Results Based Accountability Framework, Triple Bottom Line and Theory of Constraints are examples. These frameworks guide us to decide what aspects of performance are important, but they give no practical guidance on exactly how to choose and create and use the best measures to monitor performance. They are results frameworks.

PuMP

We need a deliberate measurement method, something that gives us steps to meaningfully measure what matters. PuMP is an example of that. I created it when I was the measurement consultant for Queensland Rail in the 1990s, and couldn't find any way to deal with the measurement struggles we had. I systematically tested different techniques to deal with our measurement issues. The techniques that worked became part of what I called the 'Performance Measurement Process'. It was somewhat of an epiphany to us then, to see that measuring performance was a series of steps, and not a brainstorming session. One of my colleagues, Anne, loved the 'flow' that it gave to developing measures, and she called it PuMP.

It's evolved since then, responding to the most common struggles people have with measuring performance. Some of these are:

- finding meaningful ways to measure intangible and qualitative results such as:
  — employee capability
  — culture change
  — innovation
- agreeing on the best measures for goals that are weasely and vague, e.g. 'enhance the efficiency of all we do' or 'provide unique, timely, unbiased, quality advice'
- getting buy-in and ownership of performance measures from those who will produce them and those who will use them

- helping people understand what good measures really are, and that things such as milestones and actions are not measures.

The steps of PuMP were designed to replace common practices in measuring performance that produce these struggles. In PuMP, we follow these steps:

Figure 6.1: the steps of the PuMP Performance Measure Blueprint

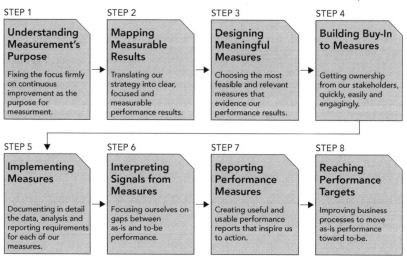

We need to integrate a measurement method such as PuMP into whatever results framework we're using. We do this by linking it in at the point of defining what our performance results are. These results might be called objectives, goals, outcomes, or even inputs and outputs. In the Balanced Scorecard, for example, this is the point at which strategic objectives are developed for the strategy map, before the strategy map is cascaded and before initiatives are developed. And in any other results framework, it's the point where goals are written to describe what the strategy aims to make a reality. We need to identify this step in whatever results framework we're using, and insert into that point a deliberate method for designing our measures.

We're using measurement, at that point, to make the results specific and observable or detectable. We're making them measurable. We're deciding what evidence would tell us to what extent those results are happening. Designing a measure for a result forces us to express that result clearly, so everyone understands it and recognises it when we bring it into reality.

We need to use a real measure design approach, a set of instructions for exactly how to get the best evidence that our result is happening. In PuMP, this happens at Step 3, with a deliberate measure design technique. It helps us deliberately convert that evidence — whether it's quantitative or qualitative — into objective measures. This is what the evidence-based leadership habit of *Evidence* means.

Is measuring performance a keystone habit?

Some habits are so powerful that, by focusing on them alone, you can start a ripple effect of other good habits with very little effort. Charles Duhigg, author of *The Power of Habit*, calls these keystone habits. There's some suggestion that measuring performance is one of these keystone habits. In his book, Duhigg talks about how a group of researchers in 2009 studied a seemingly over-simplistic approach to weight loss: at least one day a week, getting obese people to write down in a journal everything they ate.

> It was hard at first. The subjects forgot to carry their food journals, or would snack and not note it. Slowly, however, people started recording their meals once a week—and sometimes, more often. Many participants started keeping a daily food log. Eventually, it became a habit. Then, something unexpected happened. The participants started looking at their entries and finding patterns they didn't know existed...[T]his keystone habit—food journaling—created a structure that helped other habits to flourish. Six months into the study, people who kept daily food records had lost twice as much weight as everyone else.

Simply by logging data — and noticing patterns — behaviour automatically changed. No deliberate improvement actions were taken, but performance automatically improved. How interesting.

Duhigg goes on to relay the story of how Paul O'Neill, a previous CEO of Alcoa, focused the organisation on the keystone habit of safety, aiming to reduce accidents to zero. By instilling the habit of safety in everyone, from the boardroom through to the shop floor, Alcoa's performance in just about every other area dramatically improved as well — without trying.

Measuring performance is a keystone habit of the high-performance organisation. There are three reasons why:

1. *Measures focus our attention on things that matter.* When our attention is on what matters, our reticular activating system (the part of our brain responsible for conscious focus and high attention) switches on and automatically starts lining everything up, sharpening our focus to achieve what matters. Think of important personal or business goals you've measured compared to important goals you didn't measure. Where did your attention go most easily and regularly?

2. *Measures stimulate a sense of internal dissonance.* When we look at the gap between as-is and should-be (or could-be) performance in something that matters, we feel an urge to close that gap. Measures generate this competitive energy that's perfect for fuelling whatever changes are necessary to close the gap. Do you have any goals right now, where you have measured the baseline and have also set a target? How motivated do you feel to close that gap, compared to trying to reach a goal with no knowledge of the baseline and no target?

3. *Measuring our goals gives us confidence.* When we measure our goals, with objective and relevant measures we can trust, we make decisions about improvement initiatives. With confidence, we are more likely to reach our goals. We don't procrastinate, we don't hedge our bets, we're not overly risk averse. We are bolder in doing what we know needs to be done.

Evidence is the second habit of evidence-based leadership. Practising this habit in a way that encourages high performance requires three mindsets:

1. *Learning, not judging.* Use evidence to learn like a scientist learns, without judgement.
2. *Evidence before measures.* Design measures as quantifications of the observable results.
3. *Measure what matters.* Only measure what can be aligned to the priorities: mission, vision and strategic goals.

No matter what change we want to establish, and no matter how well we measure it, it will be an uphill battle if we make it about success or failure. So the first important mindset of the leadership habit of *Evidence* is about using evidence to learn like a scientist learns, without judgement.

Learning, not judging

Great performance measures:

- give us regular feedback as our strategic initiatives unfold
- are a big part of learning where the potholes that stop us from performing are, and how we can smooth them over
- are a tool to help us learn and discover and correct and adjust, before our ventures fail.

And this shift of purpose, from judging to learning, has implications for how we hold people accountable for performance.

Holding people accountable with KPIs can do more harm than good

Many leaders believe that the way to improve organisational performance is to use KPIs, or performance measures, with targets, and hold employees accountable for them. Then annually, or sometimes more frequently, these measures and targets are used in formal performance appraisals to decide on the reward or recognition or 'performance managing' that each employee needs.

We now know that using performance measures like this, in employee performance appraisal, is doing far more harm than good. Almost always, the meaningful KPIs are not within the complete control of the individual, and it leads to two negative consequences: people will either fudge the figures or scam the system. David Parmenter, in the third edition of his book *Key Performance Indicators*, says that well over half the measures used in organisations lead to these negative consequences. He calls it the 'dark side of measurement' and warns us not to underestimate how often measures can lead to worse performance. This is exactly the opposite of what we want, which is to improve performance. The measure, or KPI, becomes the focus, at the expense of bigger, and more important, outcomes.

> Using performance measures like this … is doing far more harm than good.

The traditional performance appraisal process directly clashes with many of the principles that organisations now try to emulate for high performance. We want employees to be empowered, but performance appraisal is a forced process. We want employees to collaborate, but performance appraisal focuses on individual accountability. We want employees to feel intrinsically motivated in their work, but performance appraisal motivates only with extrinsic incentives. We want employees to improve the business as a whole, but performance appraisal anchors their attention on ticking the boxes of their own job description. Even worse, Samuel Culbert, professor of Management and Organisations at UCLA's Anderson School of Management, bluntly describes the performance review as doing:

> … exactly the opposite of this intended purpose. Help people grow? Hardly. It actually prevents workers from improving. It is a dehumanising process that leaves workers demoralised, unwilling and unable to address weaknesses. It makes them hate coming to work, let alone inspires them to turn themselves into better employees.

Traditional performance appraisal is about judging people, taking a paternalistic position to 'performance manage' them by holding them to account with KPIs. And being treated like a child that can't be trusted is not the kind of environment that inspires high performance. For high performance, employees need to focus on their unique contribution to the higher purpose of the organisation.

High-performance organisations don't use measures for judging. They see measures as tools in people's hands, not rods for their backs. Any manager who adheres to paternalistic performance management will need a 180-degree turnaround before they can hold the space for a high-performance culture in their teams. And to help them make this turnaround, we have to aim our bullets right at the heart of the problem: their beliefs about how organisations and businesses change and improve.

A tool in their hands, not a rod for their back

There are several ways to help turn around these managers so they can create the kind of environment that inspires high performance.

Discuss the real consequences of measuring people

There's a good chance that the manager simply hasn't considered the causal link between measuring people and the dysfunctional behaviours that come from it. We can ask the manager how they would respond when a person's measure shows an unacceptable result. Then ask how they believe the person would feel about his response. And then ask what they expect the 'performance-managed' person realistically to do.

There will almost certainly be several examples of how people have distorted the data or distorted the process in order to make the numbers look good, rather than to find and fix performance constraints. The dysfunctional behaviours don't go away by doing more 'performance managing' (unless, of course, these employees leave the organisation). In a state of fear or defensiveness, people can't be creative. Without creativity, bold shifts in performance can't happen, and high performance is impossible.

Challenge their belief that the whole is equal to the sum of the parts

These managers believe that when people individually perform better, the whole organisation will perform better. They believe that the whole is the sum of the parts. But the truth is that the whole is more than the sum of the parts: it's the interaction among the parts. For example, competition between employees can cause problems with the end outcome (usually felt by the customer): when salespeople compete with each other to get the highest sales for the week or month, they may promise all kinds of things to customers. And the delivery team is left with the responsibility of making impossible things happen.

Check if their motivation (and priority) is to manage people or to improve company performance

Focusing too much on individual performance means losing sight of what really drives company performance. The manager needs a new definition of holding people accountable: people are accountable for using measures to continually improve business results; they are not accountable for hitting the targets for those measures. This will encourage people to keep their attention on company performance, and not just ticking the boxes of their position description.

Provide team-based approaches to achieve performance targets

What the manager wants and what 'performance-managed' people actually do are usually two very different things. We need to provide team-based approaches, such Lean Six Sigma or any process improvement method, so the manager knows exactly how to lead teams to use measures to drive performance improvement. If the team-based approach isn't easy to understand and follow, the manager will quickly go back to bad habits of judging and managing individuals.

Use case studies to show them how performance measures work best

Sometimes all it takes is to show a manager how others have succeeded using a different approach. They might only know this one way of managing performance. They've probably spent their whole career being treated the same way. Show them some alternatives, and they might just get curious about giving something different a try.

Measure results, not people

Harald is the CEO of a technology company in Germany. He adopted PuMP as his company's performance measurement approach, since he learned it at one of my workshops in Europe. As Harald led his teams through PuMP, he didn't exactly have an epiphany, but he knows he had a 180-degree turnaround in his beliefs about the use of measures to drive performance improvement. He thought measuring people on clearly defined performance measures was a fair approach to help them achieve their own objectives and let them grow, while allowing managers to objectively assess individual performance by comparing them to other people in the team.

But Harald found that when the measure showed a great result, his people regarded it as their own personal achievement. And when the measure showed a bad result, they would give him all kinds of reasons why the measure was not correct. Occasionally they would even try to manipulate the measure's result.

Harald looked for a better way to measure performance for his company, and he adopted PuMP. At first he didn't realise that PuMP was a team-based approach to measuring organisational performance, and not a method for measuring people's performance. But the principles resonated with him, and over the course of leading his team to use PuMP to measure their results, he gradually made that 180-degree turnaround.

Harald came to believe that the company should measure process results, and not measure people. He saw that when people were no longer measured they were open to improvements to the process and were motivated to contribute to the performance measurement system. He saw them buy in. Using measures to inform his people gave them the freedom to act, in contrast to measuring them, which forced them to defend themselves. Harald says:

> Now, I firmly believe that in today's world we need to put people's energy into positive actions that will lead to great results. Putting energy into defensive actions doesn't lead to anything great...The performance measures they decided to put in are now reported and discussed within the team. They don't do them for me or other managers—they do them for themselves. I can feel their intrinsic motivation for their performance measurement.

With the intrinsic motivation that comes from using KPIs as tools in their hands and not rods for their backs, employees find it much easier to feel and be accountable, but for the right things. It's too hard to practise evidence-based leadership with managers who micromanage their employees and fundamentally believe that performance only improves when people work harder. If we can't guide them through the 180-degree turnaround, we have to wait until the manager moves on, or has a performance management epiphany.

What is a KPI owner accountable for?

Let's face it: 'accountability' has been so overused in business it has become a weasel word. So what does it really mean? The dictionary definition is 'required or expected to justify actions or decisions; responsible'. If we tried to explain it to a 10-year-old, we might say something like this: if someone is accountable for something, it means they can be relied on to take care of it, and if anything goes wrong they will fix it.

Performance measures and accountability have an uncomfortable relationship. The belief is that when you are accountable for a performance measure, you will be the one who is blamed and punished if performance doesn't hit the target we set for it. So people don't like to own measures or KPIs because of the fear of what being held accountable means. And yet can performance ever be expected to improve if no-one is accountable? Of course not. So we need to sort out this uncomfortable relationship and make accountability less threatening and more compatible with improving organisational performance.

> Can performance ever be expected to improve if no-one is accountable? Of course not.

Traditionally, a measure's owner is accountable for whether or not performance hits target. If the company profit doesn't meet target, the board holds the CEO accountable. If the percentage of customer problems that are solved in the first call is too low, the customer service manager is held accountable. If the percentage of help desk calls that are answered within three rings is too low, the help desk operator is held accountable. What this means for the CEO, the customer service manager and the help desk operator is that they will be made to pay a personal price for the transgression. This price might be loss of face and humiliation, loss of privileges and opportunities, loss of bonuses and benefits, or loss of job security and self-esteem.

We know from experience the kind of behaviour this type of accountability drives. The CEO will cut costs across the board, inspiring everyone to 'work smarter'. The customer service manager will change the definition of 'solved' to get a better first-call resolution rate. The help desk operator will rush through the call she's on to answer more within three rings. And what happens in all cases is the measure will improve in the short term.

But there are consequences. Other measures will be sabotaged. Cutting costs means corners are cut and quality goes down. Changing the definition of 'solved' means problems come back into the pipeline again and cause bottlenecks. Rushing customers to end calls sooner makes them frustrated and dissatisfied.

Accountability isn't the problem. It's what we hold people accountable for when it comes to performance measures. Holding people accountable for hitting targets assumes people have full control over results, all the time. But the results are actually the product of business processes and systems, and people have to work within the constraints of these processes. W. Edwards Deming, the 'Father of Quality', had much to say about this, stating that at least 90 per cent of the constraints on performance are in the processes, not the people. And leaders own the processes.

A new accountability paradigm

For most of us, it's natural to feel threatened when we are held accountable, and we want to defend ourselves when it feels unfair. But that's not the intended outcome of accountability. The intended outcome is that the measure owner will take care of performance; they will make sure they know what it's doing and they will take the lead on improving it. It is possible to redefine accountability for performance in a more constructive way, a way that drives the right behaviour and the intended outcome of improved performance. And this constructive way has three parts to it:

1. *Hold people accountable for monitoring the important results.* When someone is responsible for a specific business result, such as problem resolution or accuracy of advice or eliminating rework, they can be accountable for routinely monitoring that result with a performance measure. They will focus on the results that matter, instead of ticking off their task list.

2. *Hold people accountable for validly interpreting their measures.* When someone is responsible for monitoring a performance measure, they can be accountable for interpreting what that measure is telling them about the business result it measures. They will seek feedback about how the results are actually tracking, instead of fudging the figures.

3. *Hold people accountable for initiating action when action is required.* When someone is responsible for interpreting a

performance measure, they can be accountable for deciding what kind of action is needed. They will work *on* their processes, not just *in* them, instead of gaming the system.

Clearly, this model of accountability for performance depends on very good measures. And very good measures are based on the strongest and most feasible evidence of the important performance results. The next mindset for practising the leadership habit of *Evidence* is about designing measures that quantify results.

Evidence before measures

Often in measuring a goal we ask a question — 'So, how do we measure that?' — too soon. As soon as we answer that question, we're doomed. The measures will be trivial counts, milestones, measures from the past, data we know we already have, the easy stuff to measure, and vague concepts that sound impressive but no-one knows how to quantify. And all these measures will have little to no strength in convincing us whether the goal is truly achieved.

When we choose performance measures properly, we never have to ask that question. A good procedure for measure selection will:

- walk us step-by-step from our goal, to its results, to the evidence of those results, to potential measures that quantify that evidence, and then to the most relevant and feasible of those measures
- start with words, not numbers
- insist that we rewrite our goals using words that make the goal come to life in our mind's eye.

And it won't be easy. We'll revert to weasel words in the blink of an eye. We'll debate about what the goal really means. We'll find it easier to talk about how to achieve the goal than how to know to what extent it is achieved. We'll list tenuous evidence of our goal. And the measures we craft from that evidence will likely be written vaguely and not quantitatively.

These are the biggest mistakes I see people make in selecting performance measures. When you're after more meaningful performance measures, use your words. We have to describe very clearly the:

- result we want to measure
- evidence of that result
- potential measures that will quantify that evidence.

Building a performance measure

Let's say we want to measure innovation. Innovation is a concept, it's not even a goal. A goal for innovation might be 'build a climate and culture of innovation'. This goal isn't clear and it isn't measurable. What exactly is a climate and culture of innovation? How is a climate different to a culture? What exactly is innovation? Perhaps this goal means that people feel motivated or compelled to generate and test ideas that bring about leaps rather than tweaks in any area of business performance. This is the first step: rewriting the goal to say what we really mean.

The next step is to get clear about the evidence that would convince us the goal was happening. The evidence might be that:

- lots of work teams have experiments on the go
- successful experiments make performance quickly increase by big margins
- not a lot of time passes between successful experiments.

And then we can quantify the evidence: create measures. The evidence could be quantified as the:

- percentage of work teams with an active experiment
- number of experiments completed per work team

- average time between the start of a successful experiment to getting a performance improvement
- average size of the shift in performance caused by successful experiments
- average time between successful experiments.

Of course we wouldn't measure all these, but by deliberately designing potential measures for the evidence of our goal, we have some very good choices. This is essentially the flow of the PuMP measure design technique. We can't take any short cuts. We have to be deliberate. The better we can use our words to write our goals and describe the evidence of them, the more meaningful our measures will be.

> The better we can use our words … the more meaningful our measures will be.

Measuring 'soft' goals

A high-ranking leader in the defence sector once asked me a question that I'm very often asked by senior leaders: How do you measure the intangible goals? He was referring to the HR and leadership and other so-called 'softer' goals that are commonly part of a strategic direction.

He chose an example from his strategic plan: 'Recruitment attracts smart candidates.' He immediately asked the right question. What does 'smart' mean? He didn't know. He hadn't thought any more deeply about it. It just sounded good when it was created during their strategy process. It's not measurable until we can agree on what we'd observe in the real world if it were already happening.

So I asked him: 'How can you tell the difference between a smart candidate and a …' He finished my question more tactfully that I was going to: '… and a not smart candidate?'

He paused for a few moments before he answered it. 'They would have a lot of the qualifications we are looking for. They would pass our entrance exams with high marks. They would be job-ready much faster than other candidates have been.'

as describing the evidence that might convince him as to a candidate was smart enough. It took another discussion like this about another of his intangible goals before he really understood what we were doing. We were making intangible things observable or detectable in the real world, and that's all we need to make them measurable. After this conversation, the world had one less leader who believed that the intangible can't be measured meaningfully.

What a good performance measure really is

Before we can successfully find meaningful performance measures, we have to know what good performance is. Just for fun, we'll start by defining what ugly performance measures are, because the flipside of what makes a measure ugly helps us define what makes a measure good.

These are examples I gathered from various businesses and organisations of so-called 'measures' for a customer service goal of 'customers love the way we serve them':

- *Win Customer Service Award.* Winning an award is a one-off or very infrequent event. Good performance measures aren't events. They are regular, ongoing, actionable feedback about the result we're trying to improve. Besides, any customer service award worth its salt would ask us how we measure our customer service performance and use those measures as part of the criteria for judging whether we deserve the award.

- *Implement Customer Relationship Management by June.* Implementing something by a due date is a milestone. Milestone achievement is simply evidence of an action, not a result. And like winning an award, it doesn't give regular and ongoing feedback that's actionable — that gives us the chance to improve performance before it's too late. Milestones are useful for project management, but they're not good measures for performance management.

- *Staff Productivity.* How is staff productivity evidence of how good customer service is? It's an ugly measure because it's just not in any way relevant evidence of the result. And besides that, it's not clear what it's even counting. It's also evidence of something other than customer service, something that could improve but at the expense of customer service. It's not a relevant measure.

- *Customer Loyalty.* Customer loyalty is too ambiguous to be a good measure. There is not a universal standard for how to calculate a measure called 'Customer Loyalty'. Loyalty means different things to different people: retention, lifetime spend with us, referral of new customers, how much they spend with us versus our competitors, and loyalty card use. Vague labels that stand alone like this don't make good performance measures.

- *Customer Survey.* A survey is a data collection method, not a measure. A customer survey collects a lot of data, data that could be used for a wide variety of potential performance measures. Perhaps this is why surveys are usually too long and not useful: people don't define the measures before working out the data they need and the best way to collect it.

In a nutshell, measures are ugly when they fail to inform us whether or not we're getting the results we wanted, and how well our actions are making those results happen. Measures are ugly when they fail to give us the feedback we need to have more influence over the results we want to create.

There are a few criteria that any measure must meet if it's going to have any chance of becoming valuable feedback for decision making.

A good measure is a quantification

Quantitative evidence is specific and comparable. To be quantitative, a measure must therefore consist of a statistic of some kind: a count, a total or sum, an average, a percentage, or a ratio. Being quantitative means we can set targets that mean something sensible, but we don't need to set a target just yet (that comes later). We just need to appreciate that a vague concept or a single number is not a performance measure. 'Recruitment targets met' is not a measure because we can't see what's counted. It becomes a measure when we write it as 'the percentage of recruitment targets that are met' or 'the average shortfall in actual recruitment numbers compared to target numbers'.

A good measure is objective

We want everyone to come to the same conclusions when they use the measure. Being objective means that the measure is not influenced by personal feelings or opinions in considering and representing facts. It means the measure is unbiased and impartial.

An objective measure is expressed by a consistent calculation using the same data, and the data is representative of the thing we're measuring. The number of customer complaints is often used as a measure of customer satisfaction, because the data is easy to get and surveys cost money. But the problem is that it's biased. Usually only customers with strong opinions or vocal personalities will voluntarily complain. Customers who have complained in the past and didn't get a response will not likely complain again. And so this measure isn't representative of all customers. It therefore tells us nothing about the level of customer satisfaction that actually exists.

A good measure is direct evidence of the goal

A measure is good evidence when it's based on directly observable facts about the goal we are measuring. A measure is bad evidence when it's really telling us about a different result. Net profit is not evidence of how satisfied customers are with our service, even though it's related; the more customer satisfaction you get, the more profit you might expect. But net profit is not a measure of customer satisfaction. The most direct measure of how satisfied customers are is something like the average rating customers give about how satisfied they are overall with our service to them.

A good measure gauges the degree to which the goal is happening

Measuring the degree of something means measuring on a continuous scale, rather than just measuring how many were a 'yes' or how many were a 'no'. For example, we can measure the degree of on-time delivery using the average number of hours late per delivery, or we can measure whether or not deliveries are late with a 'yes' or 'no' answer. If we measure average number of hours late per delivery, we are able to detect smaller changes than if we just measure the percentage that are late. This is because we can get a reduction in the number of hours late and see that result in our measure. But the percentage of deliveries that are late would change only marginally, if at all. Measures need to be sensitive enough to pick up changes in performance that are worth noticing.

> Measures need to be sensitive enough to pick up changes in performance that are worth noticing.

A good measure monitors a result

Unless we measure the results, we don't know what activities to change or how to change them. Measuring how much activity we do won't tell us this. For example, we get more insights from measuring the knowledge people retain from their training than from the number of training courses they attend. Even if we can only influence (and not have complete control over) the result, it's still more valuable to measure the actual result.

A good measure monitors routinely over time

Everything happens through time: our strategic and business planning, target setting and action plans. Unless we measure progress toward our desired results through time, we don't get a sense of whether we are heading in the right direction until it's too late.

For example, we shouldn't wait until the end of the year before we find out if our strategies succeeded at achieving our targets. We want to have the feedback in time to correct it before we miss our target altogether. Why do we measure customer satisfaction annually? It's not because it takes a long time to improve customer satisfaction; that can be done in a matter of months. Mostly it's because of the legacy of the annual customer satisfaction survey and the big costs associated with running it. Most survey data isn't used anyway, so it's a waste. It's information that's too little and too late. It can be less expensive and more informative to take a monthly pulse survey of customers. A smaller sample, with only a handful of questions, one of them being 'Overall, how satisfied are you with our service?' could be measured monthly and used as feedback throughout the year to test improvement initiatives.

The recipe for writing a quantitative measure

So how exactly do we write a good performance measure?

The trouble with writing measures with just a few words is that it leaves too much ambiguity as to how exactly it is calculated. We don't have a real measure until we've articulated how its value will be calculated. Take customer loyalty for example. We could argue that the values of this measure could be calculated in any of the following ways:

- Average number of sales per customer.
- Average number of years that a customer has been purchasing.
- Percentage of the customer base who have given repeat business.
- Average rating of likelihood that the customer will continue purchasing.
- Net Promoter Score.

We can't leave our measure calculation ambiguous like this. Chances are, the easiest thing to measure will be chosen, rather than the most meaningful thing to measure.

The solution is quite simple, and involves a four-part recipe for writing a description to accompany vague measure names.

1. *The statistic.* Decide what the best form of summary statistic is to turn the raw data into the values of our measure. We have lots of choices: number (count), total (sum), average, median, percentage, maximum, minimum, range and even more. Usually the statistic begins the description, like here:

    - *Order Turnaround Time*: Average number of days from order request to order delivery, for completed deliveries, calculated weekly.

2. *The performance attribute data.* Clearly identify the data we are applying the statistic to. What exactly are we averaging? What exactly are we counting? What exactly are we taking a percentage of? Exactly what evidence are we trying to quantify, to measure our goal? If, for example, our measure is a percentage, we really have two performance attribute data items. Take this as an example:

   • *Waste to Landfill*: Percentage of tonnes of waste produced that is sent to landfill, by month.

      — The two performance attribute data items are tonnes of waste produced and tonnes of waste sent to landfill.

3. *The scope data.* Scope data define the extent of the performance area that the measure should relate to. They define what to include in the measure, or what to exclude. Scope data items are boundaries that focus the measure. In the following measure description, the scope data is 'referred by an existing customer'.

   • *New Referred Customers*: Total number of new customers referred by an existing customer, by month.

      — You can imagine in a data set of all customers, there might be a field that flagged how the customer found out about the company. One of the values of this field could be 'existing customer' (other values might be 'web search', 'TV advertisement', etc.).

4. *The temporal data.* Contrary to popular practice, the frequency with which we measure something should not be chosen to align with reporting time frames. Just because we have a monthly report does not mean our measures' values must all be calculated monthly. The frequency of our measure should be chosen as frequent enough to detect signals as soon as possible, but not so frequent that our signals drown in noise or are diluted in the absence of data. Measures with too low a frequency tend to give very dull or delayed signals. Our chosen frequency of calculation for our measure becomes

the temporal data to include in the description, just as 'week' does here:

- *New Website Visitors*: Number of new website visitors, by week.

Is it really that simple? Well yes, and no. We need to follow this four-part recipe as the framework of describing a measure. But our measure might have a more complex calculation that needs more than one statistic, or several performance attribute data items, or a few scope data items. A good example is this measure:

- *International Training Gross Profit Margin*: Total sales revenue less total cost of sales, expressed as a percentage of total revenue, for all training workshops that are held internationally, by quarter.

With very clear and specific descriptions based on this four-part recipe, it's easier to work out what data is needed and how to turn it into the values of the performance measure. And this means we'll have a much higher chance of success in bringing our measures to life.

That begs the question: which results matter enough to measure? We'll explore this question now, and discuss the next mindset for practising the leadership habit of *Evidence*: measuring only what can be aligned to the organisation's priorities.

EVIDENCE BEFORE MEASURES

We can meaningfully measure the intangible things by describing how we'd observe or detect those intangible things playing out in the real world.

Measure what matters

To be truly evidence-based leaders, we must be curious about how well our organisation is:

- meeting its purpose
- fulfilling its mission
- achieving its vision.

Performance measures are supposed to be the evidence that convinces us we've succeeded in making these things a reality. But most of what is measured in organisations doesn't do this. We measure the:

- easy stuff: where data is readily available
- traditional stuff: what we've always measured
- obvious stuff: the resources we use, the effort we put in, and the widgets we produce
- popular stuff: the measures that everyone in our industry seems to be measuring.

What we don't measure well, or at all, is results. We don't measure the:

- outcomes
- impact
- effect
- benefits
- return on investment
- difference that our organisation is making.

We focus too much on measuring what we *do*, not the *results* of what we do. Measures of milestones and program completion are commonly found in the KPI column in strategic plans, suggesting that when the work is done, success is assumed. It suggests that we don't need to look for proof that our chosen activities have worked; we are perfect decision makers and whatever we decide upon must work.

Executives are very smart people. So are scientists. But scientists don't assume their experiments have worked without collecting the evidence to check the results of those experiments. Smart executives realise that their experience and intuition and wisdom exists as a consequence of evidence, not instead of it. Evidence informs wisdom and intuition. When we measure the results of our strategy, the results of our organisation, we're gathering some of the most powerful evidence to inform our wisdom and intuition.

The measures that matter are the ones that tell us if our decisions are making the organisation more successful. And this means we have to decide how to define 'success'.

Financial performance isn't the outcome

In the private sector, there is a strong belief that the purpose of business is to make a profit — that financial success is the ultimate measure of business success. In the public sector, the equivalent is meeting budget. In the nonprofit sector, it's attracting funding. In the majority of private and public and nonprofit organisations, these financial measures have more impact on decision making than any others.

But we don't have organisations just so we can produce a balance sheet. The National Alliance to End Homelessness doesn't exist to raise funding; it exists to eradicate homelessness, and it needs to measure how well it does that. Qantas doesn't exist to make a profit for its shareholders; it exists to safely and conveniently carry people to their desired destination, and it needs to measure how well it does that.

Every organisation has a bigger purpose than managing the finances, and every organisation should measure how well they fulfil that purpose. Financial performance is an enabler, not an outcome. Fail the purpose, and the finance is irrelevant.

Fulfilling our purpose is the outcome

Measuring our vision and mission means choosing just one or two performance measures that track our progress in making them a reality — real and objective evidence and feedback that our organisation is indeed excelling at its goals. By measuring our organisation's mission, whether it's for-profit, nonprofit or government, we take it seriously, we make it tangible and understandable, and we make it easier to align everyone's attention and goals and resources to fulfilling that mission. How can we claim that our organisation is a high-performing one if we don't have an objective measure of how well it's fulfilling its mission?

A few years ago I interviewed M. William Sermons from the National Alliance to End Homelessness (NAEH) about their deliberate and specific way of measuring their purpose. Their purpose is this:

> The Alliance works toward ending homelessness by improving homelessness policy, building on-the-ground capacity, and educating opinion leaders.

And to prove how well they are fulfilling this purpose, they used measures like these:

- Average length of time persons remain homeless.
- Median length of time persons remain homeless.
- Percentage of persons who return to homelessness.
- Number of homeless persons.
- Percentage of homeless persons who gain or increase income.
- Number of persons who become homeless for the first time.

Using measures like these, it's much easier to prove the impact that change programs have. To contribute to ending homelessness, one change program raised average incomes of people from $910 per month to more than $2000 per month within 18 months. And another change program for assisting people to remain in permanent housing exceeded its target of 75 per cent and achieved 77 per cent.

A clear and measurable mission and vision is the starting point, the inspiration, for aligning the entire organisation's measurement and execution of the strategy. And what matters next is how we measure this strategy.

Measuring strategy isn't about activity

Thanks to the physical layout of many strategic plans, milestones are confused as measures. When creating strategic plans, first strategic goals are chosen, then strategic initiatives, then targets and then, finally, the KPI or performance measure. Often, there won't even be a KPI or performance measure until after the plan is published. It's weird because, logically, we cannot choose a target until we know what we're measuring. And yet, most business plans I've seen ignore this simple logic and are laid out something like table 6.1.

Table 6.1: typical business plan

Goal	Initiatives	Target	KPI
Enhance efficiency of recruitment	Recruitment efficiency training for officers	100%	Recruitment officers educated by June

The formula they follow is:

- Vague goal.
- Initiative or list of initiatives.
- Generic targets.
- Measure (usually more action or milestones).

How can we set a target that is meaningful if we haven't decided how to measure that goal? Saying that our target is 'a 10 per cent improvement' is stabbing in the dark. Could 10 per cent be too much, or not enough, of an improvement? We don't know the measure yet so we don't know our baseline performance. Saying that we want performance to be 100 per cent is just as ludicrous. One hundred per cent of what, exactly?

It's much more sensible to set a target after we've decided that the best measure is 'average days to fill vacant positions', we've established that the baseline is 93 days and, in order to meet other business goals, it really should be reduced to 45 days. A target of 45 days for 'average days to fill vacant positions' is now a much more meaningful target.

The more logical and useful order to lay out a strategic or any plan is:

- Results.
- Measures.
- Targets.
- Initiatives.

It would look as shown in table 6.2, if we reworked the previous example.

Table 6.2: improved strategic plan

Goals	Measure	Targets	Initiatives
Enhance efficiency of recruitment	Average days to fill vacant positions	45 days	Reduce waiting time for approvals by simplifying authorisation protocols.

Following this alternative model, there are up to five essential elements that make for a results-oriented and dust-repellent strategy:

1. *Column 1: Goals.* I mean goals or objectives that are results-oriented, not weasely, and ruthlessly prioritised. They are clear statements of the outcomes that are most essential for each theme. We make them vivid, so reading the words invokes clear images of what it looks like when they're happening. We ruthlessly prioritise them, so we are only ever focused on what matters most, and only ever have a manageable number of priorities to achieve.

2. *Column 2: Measure or KPIs.* This means measures as in 'evidence', not measures as in 'we are taking measures to fix this'. Measures are quantitative values that we track regularly through time, that tell us how well we're achieving our results (from column 1). Each result only needs one or two measures, typically.

3. *Column 3: Targets.* Targets are numerical values that describe where we want our measure to be at a particular point in the future. We include for each performance measure a time-anchored target and then we have all the ingredients for a true goal or objective statement: a result (column 1) + a measure (column 2) + a target + a time frame.

4. *Column 4: Improvement Initiatives.* These are the projects, investments and opportunities we're choosing that will bring about the results we want (from column 1). To know how well these improvement initiatives are working, we'll simply look at the measures we chose (in column 2) and see if their actual values are getting closer to the target values (column 3). Many people confuse the initiatives with measures. They're not the same thing.

Evidence: Anything that matters can be measured

Sometimes strategy is 'chunked' by themes, where several results cluster together within a theme. Themes can give some structure to a strategic plan, as well as a framework for completeness or balance. We could use the Balanced Scorecard perspective, the Triple Bottom Line, or any other strategic model that takes our fancy. Irrespective of the model we use, we aim to have only three to five areas of focus — if we make it more complex, there are just more places for dust to gather. If we had used the Triple Bottom Line as our strategic planning model, our themes might be 'People', 'Profit' and 'Planet'. The previous example might then look like table 6.3.

Table 6.3: improved strategic plan, with themes

Theme	Goals	Measure	Targets	Initiatives
People	Enhance efficiency of recruitment	Average days to fill vacant positions	45 days	Reduce waiting time for approvals by simplifying authorisation protocols.

To measure what matters, we need a strategic plan that is results-oriented, that spends far more time on our person than it does on our shelf, and that means as much to us as navigational charts mean to a ship's captain. It doesn't have to be complex, glossy or an inch thick; it can be a single page. And it will make it much easier to practise the next leadership habit: *Execution*.

MEASURE WHAT MATTERS

Measure results. And measure the results that are implied by the current strategy and contribute to the fulfilment of the organisation's purpose.

CHAPTER 7

EXECUTION: IMPLEMENTING YOUR STRATEGY MUST DELIVER A HIGH ROI

Execution in high-performance organisations is keeping the organisation fit, or making it fitter, at fulfilling its purpose. It requires:

- focus on the path set by the strategic direction
- discipline to maintain that focus and take each initiative to completion
- urgency, to make sure the whirlwind of day-to-day operations doesn't sabotage the change effort
- leverage, to get the highest return possible from the investment of our limited time, effort and money.

What we're doing in practising the habit of *Execution* is implementing change initiatives that can take a big bite out of our performance gaps, closing as much of the gap between current performance and targeted performance as possible.

Execution means improvement

The Federal Aviation Administration (FAA) in the US wanted to reduce the time it took to find placements for those people who didn't pass the flight controller's exam (referred to as 'training failures'). They measured the Training Failure Processing Time: the average number of days between failing the exam and taking up a new placement. Training Failure Processing Time was sitting at an overall average of 67 days, but from month to month it varied chaotically between 40 and 110 days. This meant a lot of lost productivity as the people who failed the exam waited for alternative assignments, and a lot of angst for those people as they waited in limbo to find out whether they had a job and, if so, where that job was going to be. The leaders set a target of 30 days.

To reach the target, they began by examining the 'as-is' training failure placement process. They worked with field managers to brainstorm what they thought was delaying the process and gathered complaints from the employees and the union. They discovered that much of the time taken to process training failures was spent waiting: waiting for responses, waiting for approvals, waiting for the failed air traffic control specialists to make their decisions about alternative placements. So, they redesigned the process. In doing so, they sought and won support from both the unions and management.

The improvement saw Training Failure Processing Time drop to 23 days, so they went ahead and set the next target at 14 days. This improvement reduced lost productivity and saved nearly $500 000 over the seven-month period during which the improvements were made. To make the improvement, they had spent $12 000 on team training and time away from their usual jobs. The ROI, therefore, was ($500 000 − $12 000) ÷ $12 000 — a staggering 4067 per cent.

Jack Phillips writes a lot about how to measure change, and the importance of measuring the ROI of change. The cornerstone of

his model of measuring any change is a framework of five le
quantifiable results:

1. *Reaction.* What people think, feel or believe about their experience of the change.

2. *Learning and knowledge.* What people have learned as a result of the change.

3. *Implementation and behaviour.* What people have done or completed as part of the change.

4. *Business impact.* The shifts or trends in important business performance measures as a result of the change.

5. *ROI.* The net benefit made by the change.

Most organisations will stop at level 3. They think that level 4 is a struggle, and level 5 is all but forgotten about. It's little wonder that we don't truly know the leverage we're getting from our strategy execution. And if we don't know, it's almost a certainty that the ROI is nowhere near as high as it could be. Measuring ROI is not negotiable for a high-performance organisation.

> Measuring ROI is not negotiable for a high-performance organisation.

Execution is the habit of basing strategy implementation on high-ROI improvement initiatives. But finding that high ROI requires a few mindset shifts:

- *Leverage, not force.* Implement or execute strategy based on working smarter, not harder.

- *Patterns, not points.* Make strategy execution about removing and managing variability, not about hitting the numbers.

- *Processes, not people.* Execute strategy to improve business processes and how work is designed, not to control people and what work is done.

We've started talking about leverage already, but it's also important to know what it's replacing. This first mindset for practising the evidence-based leadership habit of *Execution* is about implementing or executing strategy based on working smarter, not harder.

Leverage, not force

Archimedes was an Ancient Greek mathematician, physicist, engineer, inventor, and astronomer. In explaining the concept of leverage, his famous quote is, 'Give me a lever long enough and a fulcrum on which to place it and I shall move the world.'

Leverage is everywhere. The cranks on a bicycle. A golf club held in our hands. A beer bottle opener. The seesaw in a children's playground. Leverage is the principle that makes hard things easy. The leverage that Archimedes spoke of applies just as appropriately to how we lead high-performance organisations. Archimedes' 'world' is the result we want our organisation to create; and this is our first habit of *Direction*, articulated through our corporate strategy. Archimedes' 'fulcrum' is how we measure that result — our second habit of *Evidence* — so we can base our action on a stable foundation of fact. The lever is our improvement initiative — the action we have chosen, informed by our measure — to reach our goal.

To improve performance, to increase our business's capacity for excellence, requires leverage. If an improvement can only be sustained by continually putting in more effort, there's no leverage. If we give a team a target to increase their output by 20 per cent, they will ask for 20 per cent more people or more budget in order to hit that target. But we want the increase in output without having to pay continuously for it. We want the team to find their untapped potential and use that to increase their output. What we want is leverage.

> If an improvement can only be sustained by continually putting in more effort, there's no leverage.

A sugar mill, a major customer of the railway I used to work for, was increasing its production and required our freight business to increase its capacity to move more sugar from the mill to the port for export. The freight business looked at its traditional financial reports, carefully ran scenarios with the numbers, and worked out how much they could spend on additional capacity and still make a profit. Their solution was to invest millions of dollars into more trains and wagons in order to meet the demands of increased sugar production. But the freight manager wasn't convinced that investing in trains and wagons was the most meaningful way to do it: it merely compensated for an operations process that wasn't making the best use of the resources it already had. It lacked leverage.

The best solution was startling. It required no additional investment at all, it improved cycle times, met more than the mill's planned production increases, and even reduced the operating expense. The solution identified an incredible amount of waste in the freight process and transformed the process to better serve the customer and produce greater profit for the rail company.

The solution was to change the way that trains were used to move the sugar from mill to port. Rather than doing what railways always did — which was to receive production numbers from the customer each week and then put together trains of appropriate length and schedules of appropriate frequency — the solution involved using unit-length trains (trains with a set number of wagons) that cycled continuously from mill to port. And these unit-length trains were designed to have one wagon more than they needed, as a buffer. This buffer wagon became a powerful performance indicator for the system. When the buffer wagon was needed to carry additional sugar, this was a lead indicator that mill production was ramping up again, which gave the railway company time to adjust the system to meet the increased production so that freight transport would not become a bottleneck for the sugar mill. The freight process was made fundamentally better because this solution fixed the real root causes constraining performance: outdated policies and practices.

This solution showed that the policies that had always been in place, the practices that were always accepted as right, were constraining performance. It showed that the capacity of the rail system was constrained by system design, not resources or effort.

It's usually desperation that drives this tendency to use effort rather than leverage. Everyone can try harder immediately. But usually they have to *keep* working harder, because if they slacken off again, performance drops. Leverage requires some time to finesse a solution, but it's the kind of solution that is implemented once and continues to elevate performance. Culturally, we know this. We talk about 'sharpening the saw', 'a stitch in time saves nine', and 'an ounce of prevention is worth a pound of cure'.

Humans — including leaders — often have a blind spot when it comes to interpreting data properly and lack the patience to wait for enough data that can reveal the truth about performance, what is constraining it, and what works in lifting those constraints. For measures of performance to be the fulcrums they should be to help us find leverage in our actions, we have to learn how to use them properly to decide when to act, and whether our actions worked. The next mindset of practising the evidence-based leadership habit of *Execution* is making strategy execution about removing and managing variability, not about hitting the numbers.

LEVERAGE, NOT FORCE

To improve performance, to increase our business's capacity for excellence, we need leverage. If an improvement can only be sustained by continually putting in more effort, we didn't find the leverage.

Patterns, not points

When the freight manager modelled the sugar freight system, he gathered data about how the process worked and then built a simulation of it. It wasn't a theoretical exercise; he made that model match reality so well that it behaved in a very similar way to how the actual freight system was behaving. The most important part of his approach was to work with variability, not just averages. He collected data about the:

- average sugar production and the typical variability in sugar production

- average loading time of sugar onto the trains, and the typical variability in loading time
- average transit time of the trains, and the typical variability in transit time
- average unloading time of sugar at the port, and the typical variability in unloading time.

Every step of the sugar freight system, and data about how it behaved, was captured in the model.

Patterns of variability

Variation is fundamentally important to understanding how things work together in a system. When we drive on the highway, we're often flabbergasted by stop–start traffic that seems to have no cause. There are no accidents blocking lanes. The highway isn't any busier than it usually is. There are no roadworks with speed restrictions. Why then, does the traffic slow to a stop and then suddenly, miraculously, speed up again?

The answer is variability. The presence of variability in any process causes dynamics that can sometimes be hard to predict. The variability in the speed that a driver holds can cause the driver behind them to make a small change in their own speed, which adds to their own variability in speed. And this in turn affects the driver behind them. And so on. Usually this variability in speed is buffered by the space we allow between our cars, and our ability to anticipate and change lanes. The entire highway system works because most of the time it sits within a state of equilibrium — 'business as usual', we might say. But a small and unusual change can unsettle the equilibrium. Like a broken-down car parked on the side of the highway. Suddenly the majority of drivers are rubber-necking, which is enough to increase the normal variability in speed of most drivers on the highway. And the buffer is no longer enough to absorb it. Drivers start using their brakes to compensate, and the domino effect flows back up the highway. The system's performance, average speed in this case, suffers.

When we can understand the patterns of variability in our own business systems, we can learn so much more about their performance. Averages don't tell the whole story; they are like a photograph. But variability tells a richer story; it's the movie. It's the patterns we need to look for, not the points. And it's a mindset shift.

Keep the big picture in the frame

Lots of leaders share the same bad habit: they conclude whether performance is getting better or worse by comparing the current month's (or week's or quarter's) performance measure value with last month's, or with a target or standard. If this month (or week or quarter) is worse, they go digging for the cause. Trouble is, they don't find that cause.

I've noticed when riding my mountain bike, if I look too close in front of me, about a metre or two, every rock, log, rut and patch of loose pebbles looks like something I need to correct for. Paying so much attention to these short-term obstacles makes me try too hard to control where my front wheel goes, and I end up correcting so much that I can get the wobbles, and down I go. But if I instead look further ahead, paying attention to the bigger picture of 10 to 30 metres in front of me, the bike tracks more smoothly. When it hits one of those rocks or ruts or patches of loose pebbles, it's no big deal. We just move through them, and keep going forward. As my riding skill increases and my fitness improves, I can absorb more of these obstacles and they have less effect on my control of the bike. Overall, my mountain bike riding experience moves to a higher level of performance and, interestingly, it does so with less effort. I can more easily pinpoint specific skills or behaviours that I can sharpen and hone. Focusing on the bigger picture helps me find leverage.

> Focusing on the bigger picture helps me find leverage.

Those leaders with the bad habit of comparing this month to last month haven't found the causes of their so-called performance dips, because the causes don't exist. They might blame things akin to rocks or logs or ruts or patches of loose pebbles. Performance isn't actually getting worse; there are always little obstacles that make our ride less than perfectly smooth and predictable. Most of the time, when I do a proper time-series analysis of their performance measures, it proves that overall nothing has really changed.

Here's one example: train derailments. It's used in every railway organisation around the world to measure the number of times that trains come off the rails. In figure 7.1 we can clearly see that train derailments, for this particular railway, do indeed vary from month to month. But that pattern of variability, over a long period of time, is very stable and therefore predictable. Performance hasn't changed at all.

Figure 7.1: train derailments are variable, but stable

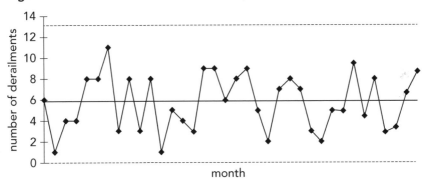

Here's the real problem: When we look only at the short term, we end up over-correcting and tampering, making variability worse — and increased variation is the enemy of high-performance.

The entire field of quality and process improvement — which has revolutionised many industries over the last 60 or so years — centres on managing the factors that cause controllable variation in performance, so we can get more control (or at least influence) over that performance.

We need to look longer term and understand the natural variation in our business results, and learn about the factors that have the most impact on the variation's size. We need to keep our eyes on the big picture. It's the patterns, not the points, that show us the leverage for improving performance. This is statistical thinking.

Statistical thinking powers evidence-based leadership

Statistical thinking is not so much about having knowledge of, and being able to apply, statistical techniques. It's not about knowing how to perform a regression analysis or knowing the formula for putting a trend line through a time series. We don't have to be a statistician or a numbers person to master statistical thinking. Statistical thinking is simply about understanding a few basic concepts.

> We don't have to be a statistician or a numbers person to master statistical thinking.

All things vary

The first concept is that all things vary. Everything varies, seemingly erratically, due mostly to complexity and the interactions among many causal factors. Speed on the highway varies because of our accelerator pedal control, our engine's responsiveness, how much time we spend looking around versus looking ahead. Sales vary because of the economy, marketing message, amount of marketing activity, what's happening in the lives of your target market, even the weather. Workplace accidents, office supply expenses, satisfaction of customers, our weight from day to day: everything goes up and down with random but very natural and often predictable variation caused by the complex interplay of the factors that affect it.

Uncertainty is unavoidable

The second concept of statistical thinking is that, because things vary, there is uncertainty. We can't ever really know anything 100 per cent. Statistics is not like mathematics, where you get exact answers when you combine numbers in a formula, and neither is the world. The world is inherently uncertain and variable. Statistics is the study of uncertainty and variability, and its core purpose is to see pertinent patterns in our data. We don't know exactly how many sales we'll get next week because we don't know how all the causal factors in the universe will play out to affect it. But we could predict it within a range, based on what we've observed historically.

Measure the uncertainty

The key to knowing something is to find measures of uncertainty. This makes signals stand out. We can look to the past to see how much sales have varied from week to week so we can estimate next week's sales within a likely range. This is why the concept of variation is fundamental to statistics. Variation measures the uncertainty. This routine variation is fundamental to how we can draw knowledge from data because it helps us gauge the amount of uncertainty inherent in whatever it is we want to measure and manage.

Managing using statistical thinking

Managers at a timber sawmill had a performance dashboard that tracked a bunch of measures about how sawmill operations were performing. The data for these figures refreshed every few minutes. Traffic lights — the usual red, green, and amber that flags when performance is bad, good, or heading toward unacceptable — were also updated each time the data feed refreshed. The managers and supervisors would react to these traffic lights, changing the settings on timber processing equipment or altering procedures, to move performance back into acceptable ranges. They believed they had a very sophisticated performance management system. But performance just wasn't improving. In fact, it seemed to be getting worse. They were repeating the same mistake, failing over and over again with each initiative to improve performance.

What was happening was not visible to them. Those traffic lights they trusted so much changed based on data from a small sample, often just a single day. The feedback they were getting about their milling system was suddenly sped up to a cadence that was much faster than the natural cadence of change in the milling system. The dashboard didn't show them longer-term trends or the natural variability in the data. The faster cadence showed them only random noise, not clear signals, so they were reacting to any variation in the data at all. Everyone was so busy reacting to data that they couldn't see what really needed to be fixed. Changing what was working fine, coupled with ignoring what needed fixing, is why performance worsened.

Executives eventually realised that the dashboard was causing everyone to tamper with the production processes. The dashboard was removed from the site, and almost immediately, performance began to stabilise and improve.

What we need to manage is the *pattern of variation*, not the points of data! The implication for us, and for combining the evidence-based leadership habits of *Evidence* and *Execution*, is that we *cannot* find knowledge in individual points of data. Knowledge can come only from patterns in data. And these patterns are patterns of variation. If the variation reduces or increases or moves, it generally is a signal that something happened to cause a change. And when the pattern of variation doesn't change, it is also a signal that our efforts are likely having no effect.

We cannot lead a high-performance organisation, we cannot practise evidence-based leadership, without statistical thinking. When we ignore variation and uncertainty, we react to every fluctuation as though it means something significant happened that we must react to. But far more often than not, nothing significant has happened. Those fluctuations are just a natural product of complex and interrelated causes. And reacting to them only adds complexity and increases the variation.

> When we ignore variation and uncertainty, we react to every fluctuation.

So how do we know when something significant happened in a KPI? How do we know when we need to take action to improve performance? We need to distinguish the routine and natural variation in our performance data from the abnormal or non-routine variation that signals a change. And it's easy to do this — even though most people don't know about it. It takes just your KPI data, a few easy calculations, and one simple graph called an XmR chart.

The signals of performance are in the patterns

We won't find true signals of changes in performance by looking at month-to-month comparisons, or trend lines, or moving averages. The signals we really need to know about, the only signals that you ought to respond to, are revealed through XmR charts.

Figure 7.2: the timber company's measure of throughput

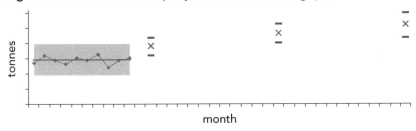

The jagged up-and-down line in figure 7.2 is the performance measure of timber throughput: the tonnes of timber products manufactured that are within specification. The solid horizontal line is the central line, and is basically telling us where current performance is for timber throughput, despite its variability. The shaded range is the natural process limits, which tell us how much variation is typical for timber throughput. The x-marks and dashes that are above and below them are targets. These targets represent the growth in timber production that is expected over the coming years, that the site manager has to find the capacity to manufacture. The x-marks are targets for the average amount of timber to manufacture, and the upper and lower dashes are targets for the variability in the amount of timber to manufacture.

The site manager would change various parameters to see what effect they might have on timber throughput. He and his production team might test a few solutions, like changing inventory levels or cross-training employees to operate different machines. And they would monitor to see which solutions had the best impact.

The solutions that tested best would be implemented, and we might see something like the pattern shown in figure 7.3 (overleaf).

Execution: Implementing your strategy must deliver a high ROI

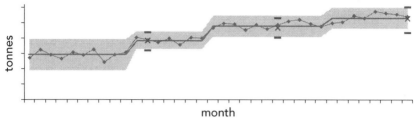

Figure 7.3: timber throughput improving enough to meet targets

The XmR chart takes our attention off the individual points of our measures and directs it to the patterns in our measures' variability. It filters the noisy routine variation in our measures by showing us how much of this routine variation there is, by way of the natural process limits. And coupled with the central line, these natural process limits give us a meaningful baseline to quickly assess when performance has changed — when there is something else going on that's not part of the routine variation.

> The XmR chart takes our attention off the individual points of our measures and directs it to the patterns in our measures' variability.

XmR charts take only a little effort to create, but they make the practice of evidence-based leadership so much easier. They open the door to strategy execution that is based on leverage, not force — on strategy execution that achieves stretch targets. (For more information on using XmR charts, please refer to appendix A.)

Targets are about capability improvement, not hitting numbers

A typical way to set targets is to calculate a target for the year, and then apportion it to each month in that year. The idea is to keep everyone focused on achieving the target, thereby increasing the likelihood the annual target will be met.

But it doesn't work. These targets are typical of sales teams, where each month the sales reps will chase a quota to contribute toward hitting the annual goal. The example in table 7.1 shows how monthly targets are apportioned 'realistically' throughout the year. The sum of these values is the annual target (it's $14 000 000, in case you're burning to know). Negative values are where actual performance was under target for the month.

Table 7.1: sales revenues vs targets

	Sales Revenue ('000)		
	Target	Actual	Difference
Jul 12	$850	$876	$26
Aug 12	$900	$880	−$20
Sep 12	$950	$811	−$139
Out 12	$1 000	$909	−$91
Nov 12	$1 050	$1 187	$137
Dec 12	$1 100	$1 111	$11
Jan 13	$1 150	$828	−$322
Feb 13	$1 200	$934	−$266
Mar 13	$1 300	$904	−$396
Apr 13	$1 400	$1 101	−$299
May 13	$1 500	$975	− $525
Jun 13	$1 600	$1 289	−$311

There will almost always be negative values, unless the current capability of the revenue-generating process is already well above the target. The negative values are simply a product of natural variability. Every measure will always vary to some extent, resulting from the interplay of a huge array of causes, including both the external environment and the design of internal business processes.

Increasing capability to consistently generate more revenue requires changing the design of the business processes that contribute to revenue. Sales — the process of turning a lead into a customer — is just one of those business processes. Marketing — the process of identifying potential top accounts and getting their attention — is another of those business processes.

But while sales staff focus on hitting monthly targets, they won't have the time or awareness to work on the business processes — they'll only do what they can to hit the current month's target. We've all heard about the old sales tricks: big discounts (that aren't profitable), bullying customers (and destroying long-term relationships), counting promised sales (that never come through).

A better way is to use targets to improve capability, not hit monthly quotas. The following is an XmR chart of revenue (see figure 7.4), with a target point sitting above the date by which it is to be achieved. It's the same data as in table 7.1, but with a bit more of the historical data included, back to January 2011.

Figure 7.4: sales revenue in an XmR chart

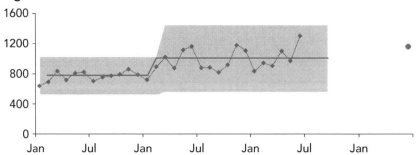

The target for the XmR chart was calculated by dividing the annual target into 12, given that the measure is calculated monthly. This target is where we want the central line to get to, ideally well before June. Currently the revenue-generating capability is about $1 million per month, and the target is $1.17 million. Apart from the signal of an upward shift back in January (who knows what caused that), there is no signal whatsoever that revenue is increasing enough for that central line to move up to the target. The sales reps might be working their little bums off, but the capability of the sales process is holding them down.

Think of a supercharged V8 street car racing the quarter mile: it's not ever going to consistently produce 12-second runs until the processes of that car increase their capability: engine capacity, fuel mixture, engine timing, tyre traction and so on. Driving harder won't achieve it, not without the risk of blowing up the engine by over-revving it.

Chasing targets by focusing on hitting a number each and every month encourages behaviours that are usually unsustainable, too:

- Working faster.
- Working longer.
- Trying harder.
- Going for quick wins that might sabotage other areas of performance (such as customer relationships or staff retention).

Staff continually need to inject more effort to keep hitting monthly numbers.

But when we pursue a capability target, such as the target for the XmR central line, our focus is on increasing the capability of our underlying business processes. Improve the business process design once, and we get a sustainable increase in capability that doesn't cost any further effort. For every process improvement we make, we get another ongoing capability improvement that sustains itself. It's bigger gains for less effort (a good definition of leverage, actually).

Isn't that what performance measurement and improvement is really about? And that's why we need to take our attention off the targets we set for people, and put our attention on improving process capability. Therefore, the next mindset of practising the evidence-based leadership habit of *Execution* is about executing strategy to improve business processes and how work is designed, not about controlling people and what work is done.

PATTERNS, NOT POINTS

We can only understand performance by understanding the patterns of variability in performance. Averages only tell a static story, like a photograph; but variability shows a movie. It's the patterns we need to look for, not the points.

Processes, not people

When we build a dynamic model of a system, like the freight manager did for the sugar system, we can change various parameters to see what effect they might have on a specific performance measure. The sugar system model was built with actual data about the:

- length of the track
- schedule of trains
- lengths and capacities of the trains
- variation in the train transit times
- variation in the sugar loading and unloading times
- expected delays at the mill and at the port
- capacity of ships at the port

and so on. The freight manager played with these parameters, including the solution of investing in more rolling stock, to see which solution had the best impact. What he was playing with was the design of the sugar freighting business process, the flow of steps of moving sugar from mill to port.

Most measures don't improve performance because we don't have the discipline to do the fundamental cause analysis required for us to find the leverage. Our actions focus on easy fixes, such as educating people, writing policies, or buying more trains and wagons: 'We have to do some customer education', 'we need a policy for that', 'we need to increase our rolling stock by 20 per cent'. No, we probably don't.

> Most measures don't improve performance because ... our actions focus on easy fixes.

We need to get to the root of what's going on and focus on the capability of our business processes. What can we fundamentally change in the process to get the outcome that we want? If customers aren't paying our bills, they don't need education in how to pay bills; we probably need a better billing process that:

- is easier
- gets the bill to them quickly enough so that they've got plenty of time to pay

- makes it much simpler for customers to understand:
  — how much they've got to pay without surprises
  — when they've got to pay it by
  — what the payment options are.

Process improvement methods such as Lean Six Sigma and Business Process Re-engineering, and modelling tools such as the one used for the sugar system, couple very well with performance improvement and strategy execution. They provide a disciplined approach to diagnose and improve process capability. They help us to look at how we've designed the process and show us how to streamline that process to remove waste and reduce the opportunities for problems to occur. Coupled with our performance measures, process improvement gives us a way to remove the causes of unacceptable performance, not just compensate for it with Band-Aids and painkillers.

Measuring people's performance is often what leaders think performance measurement is. They don't think about measuring organisational or process performance. Too many people want to know how to make measuring people easier, more engaging and more meaningful.

Simple answer: we can't, so stop measuring people. Instead, let people collaboratively measure process performance. After all, most of the constraints that are holding performance back are in how business processes are designed, and rarely ever in the people.

Problems are in the process, not the people

Leaders, managers and human resource professionals all want to know how to cascade company goals to individuals, and put measures in their performance agreements. It's the toughest question I am ever asked, because my answer isn't what leaders want to hear. The way that I learned that 90 per cent of the problems are in the process and not the people was through training in Six Sigma, Total Quality Management and other process improvement methods in general.

The quality movement of the 1950s and onward was led by W. Edwards Deming, the 'Father of Quality'. Deming had a lot to say on the topic of measuring people. In *Total Quality Management*, the authors Dale H. Besterfield and others describe Deming's approach as:

> …management by numerical goal is an attempt to manage without knowledge of what to do.

From Deming's own works *The New Economics*:

> A manager of people needs to understand that all people are different. This is not ranking people. He needs to understand that the performance of anyone is governed largely by the system that he works in, the responsibility of management…
>
> When the system is stable, telling a worker about mistakes is only tampering.

And my personal favourites, from *Out of the Crisis*:

> Evaluation of performance, merit rating, or annual review…The idea of a merit rating is alluring. The sound of the words captivates the imagination: pay for what you get; get what you pay for; motivate people to do their best, for their own good. The effect is exactly the opposite of what the words promise…

From Deming's introduction to *The Team Handbook*:

> The fact is that the system that people work in and the interaction with people may account for 90 or 95 percent of performance.

The downward spiral

When we use performance measures to focus on managing *people's* performance rather than *process* performance, it makes performance worse. It reinforces a downward spiral in overall organisational performance:

- *It starts with monitoring.* Managers want people to perform better so they monitor people to assess their performance.
- *Monitoring leads to judgements.* When people know they are being monitored, they feel judged. Do you like to feel judged?

- *Judgements lead to threats.* People will then take the judgements personally and that makes them feel threatened.
- *Threats lead to defensiveness.* When people feel threatened, they get defensive in an attempt to protect themselves. The most common method to protect themselves from the threat of performance measures is to hide performance problems so the measures look good. Or they will manipulate the measures to make the results look good. Or they will set targets for measures they know they can achieve.
- *Defensiveness makes performance worse.* When the important performance problems are hidden, performance gets worse. Why wouldn't it get worse if it's being ignored?
- *Worsening performance leads to more monitoring.* Managers will pick up that performance is worsening, and so their instinct is that more monitoring is needed.

More monitoring means that people are feeling the scrutiny of more judgement. And the spiral continues to go down.

Is this pattern familiar to you? What have you noticed happens when you measure people to monitor how they perform? Have you seen it work consistently well? Can you produce sufficient convincing evidence that measuring people is the best way to reach organisational goals? It's not likely.

Adopting the belief that at least 90 per cent of the problems are in the process and not in the people is central to the ability of organisations to make great progress in improving productivity, quality and financial performance. They focus on measuring and improving processes and, rather than treating employees as an asset to get a return from, they treat them as people. They give them opportunities to learn and grow and apply their skill and creativity to collaboratively make the processes better.

It's not that we can't measure a person's performance. We can measure anything at all if we can frame it as an observable result. The contention I have is more about *when* it's helpful to measure a person's performance, and *how* we go about doing it. I detest the idea of treating someone like an organisational asset, something we are trying to control. Leaders need to create the conditions and remove the constraints so that people can perform, not set up systems to force performance out of them.

But measures can certainly help individuals to improve their personal performance — when those measures are chosen and used by the individual, not chosen by someone else and used to judge the individual. It's simply a matter of the individual deciding what their goals or desired results are, and how they'll monitor them.

That said, it still stands to reason that if 90 per cent of performance problems are in the process, wouldn't we want to master the measurement of processes first, before worrying about measuring people?

Executing strategy means improving processes

One essential reason that we have organisations in the first place is that something needs to get done again and again for a particular group of stakeholders or customers. This thing that needs to get done happens through a process: roads being built in our cities, or illnesses being diagnosed and cured, or apples being available at the supermarket, or policies being developed. In other words, work actually happens through a series of steps or activities that flow together as a process.

Here's the kicker: how well our processes are designed directly determines how well we do the thing our organisation is supposed to do. It's *process* performance that has the biggest impact on organisational success, not *people* performance. So process performance is too important not to measure. Then naturally, our change initiatives — our practice of *Execution* — needs to be directed at improving processes.

> It's *process* performance that has the biggest impact on organisational success, not *people* performance.

We're not going to know what to measure or improve about our organisation's processes until we first figure out what our processes are, and what results they produce that most affect our organisation's success. One of the best ways to figure out our processes is to start with our customers, and name the outputs we produce for them. Then for those outputs, we map backwards to find the flows of activities and steps that produce those outputs. We flowchart all the way back to the very trigger that sets that process into action. Mostly it's when the customer asks for our service or product.

The great thing about using processes as the framework to identify our performance measures is that we build a natural diagnostic system of measures — evidence about how well important things are actually happening. The measures of outcomes tell us how the process is going in general. But rarely do they tell us how to *improve* process performance. That's where the in-process measures come into their own: the measures of critical activities within processes. They are measures that give us the clues about what to fix to improve performance.

Program logic models visually map these cause–effect relationships that exist between the inputs, activities and outputs, and outcomes associated with a change initiative. They provide a framework for assessing the impact achieved by the change initiative. For example, a regional council might map the logic of a water-saving program as shown in figure 7.5.

Figure 7.5: program logic for a water-saving program

PROGRAM GOAL: Reduce water consumption in the community.

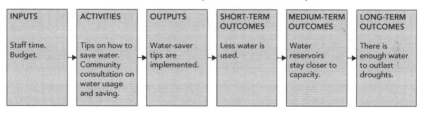

These models are intended for organisations whose impact is social change, such as reducing health problems from smoking, reducing water consumption in times of drought, increasing use of sunscreen to minimise skin cancer incidence, or reducing homelessness. But the input-activity-output-outcome thinking that program logic frameworks encourage is very helpful in general for cascading strategy into processes, not just functional areas. For example, an electricity company's procurement department might align their process and sub-processes to the corporate strategy as shown in figure 7.6.

Figure 7.6: program logic models cascade strategy into processes

STRATEGIC GOAL: Decrease operating costs.

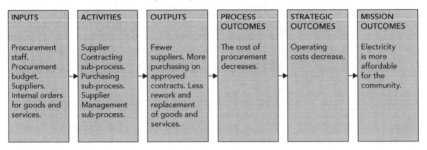

INPUTS	ACTIVITIES	OUTPUTS	PROCESS OUTCOMES	STRATEGIC OUTCOMES	MISSION OUTCOMES
Procurement staff. Procurement budget. Suppliers. Internal orders for goods and services.	Supplier Contracting sub-process. Purchasing sub-process. Supplier Management sub-process.	Fewer suppliers. More purchasing on approved contracts. Less rework and replacement of goods and services.	The cost of procurement decreases.	Operating costs decrease.	Electricity is more affordable for the community.

A strategy that cascades corporate goals into process goals, and builds on a diagnostic system of measures, is the best approach to find the leverage that defines high-performance organisations. It helps everyone working in the organisation to clearly see the impact of their own work on performance, and trace that impact all the way up to organisational performance. It makes it easier for everyone to work together in unison, to execute strategy and achieve high performance.

PROCESSES, NOT PEOPLE

It stands to reason that if at least 90 per cent of performance problems are in the process, we must master the measurement of processes, and their outputs and outcomes.

PART II
IN SUMMARY

Part II has been about the habits we need to lead high-performance organisations: *Direction, Evidence* and *Execution*.

The habit of *Direction* is about setting strategic goals that are written as plainly and clearly as possible, in a way that people at all levels will truly understand and that is meaningfully measurable. They must be:

- results-oriented, not activities
- clear and specific, not weasely
- ruthlessly prioritised, not business as usual.

The habit of *Evidence* is about measuring our strategy in a way that helps us learn what truly works, by measuring important results directly and quantitatively, and only measuring the important results. Measures work when they are used for learning, not judging. We can only meaningfully measure what we can observe or detect in the real world. And we should only measure what truly matters in the context of our strategy.

The habit of *Execution* is about finding the leverage to achieve stretch targets for our strategy, and finding this leverage in the understanding, measurement and improvement of our business processes. We want to make fundamental performance improvements, where we can fix it once and it stays fixed. We don't want to be distracted by normal variation, and waste effort tampering with things that aren't broken. Our efforts are focused on how to improve our business processes, not monitor our people, since that's where almost all performance problems will be.

PART III
ORGANISATIONAL HABITS OF EVIDENCE-BASED LEADERSHIP

Evidence-based leaders practise specific habits, as explored in part II, but they also inspire high-performance habits organisation-wide. These evidence-based organisational habits are *Decision, Action* and *Learning*.

- *Decision* is about helping people take ownership for the results that matter by:
  — giving them a clear line of sight to the corporate strategy
  — getting their honest buy-in
  — giving them authority to work on the business.
- *Action* is about helping people discover how to achieve the results that matter through a focus on:
  — causal analysis
  — practicality
  — collaboration.
- *Learning* is about helping people make working on the business a normal part of their work by:
  — adopting an experimental mindset
  — learning from failure
  — iterating the way to success.

In high-performance organisations, these habits are practised by everyone. Evidence-based leaders make it clear that these habits are important, by visibly mastering *Direction, Evidence* and *Execution*. The trigger to start the practice of the organisational habits is to cascade the strategy so that everyone can feel ownership of it.

CHAPTER 8

DECISION: THEY WANT TO WORK FOR SOMETHING BIGGER THAN THEMSELVES

When I work with executive teams to make their strategy measurable, by the time we've made it results-oriented and de-weaselled it, we often realise that many of the goals are in fact multifocused. What starts out as six strategic goal statements becomes 15 or more individual performance results. Local government often encounters this problem: strategy is written so broadly that it unpacks into an unmanageable (and very un-strategic) number of true goals. One regional council had eight strategic themes — their highest-level goals. When we unpacked just the first of these eight strategic themes, by making sure it was about results and by translating the weasel words, we ended up with 15 specific performance results. Imagine how overwhelmed the team felt when they realised this was only the first goal.

Decision means focus

The evidence-based leadership habit of *Direction* involves being ruthless. In *The 4 Principles of Execution* the authors advise us to focus on just a few 'wildly important goals'. As leaders, we must do this when we set the organisational direction. And as leaders we must inspire this focus on the wildly important throughout the whole organisation.

The CEO of a small company that helps car dealerships automate their sales processes played the perfect role in inspiring such focus when all nine of his business divisions used PuMP to develop new KPIs. The first few steps of PuMP have each team get very clear about their goals and design measures for them. Then, before they take the next steps of bringing those measures to life and using them, they have what's called a Measures Gallery.

> The evidence-based leadership habit of *Direction* involves being ruthless.

A Measures Gallery is like an art gallery, where the art is the newly designed measures. It's held in a meeting room or open space, with no chairs or tables or PowerPoint. The team's goals and measures — and the completed PuMP templates that designed them — hang on the walls. There'll also be some snacks or treats for visitors to enjoy. It's a space for dialogue, not agendas. There are no start times or finish times, just opening hours. Most Measures Galleries are open for a half to a full day. Dozens or hundreds of people are invited — anyone who might have an interest or a stake in the measures. They come and go, if and as they please. While they're at the Gallery, they talk with each other about the team's goals and measures and share their constructive ideas, suggestions, corrections, questions and encouragement.

The CEO of the dealership support company visited every one of the nine Measures Galleries. He spent just 10 minutes or so asking the team to tell the story of their goals and how they linked back to his strategic direction. He asked questions, he challenged their thinking, and he guided them in selecting the three most important goals. He helped them focus on their most powerful contribution to the company's strategy.

As evidence-based leaders, we role-model *Decision* by being ruthless when we practise the habit of *Direction*. We set just a few strategically important goals, and commit to them. Because we want the whole organisation focused on achieving excellence in the few results that matter most, we must also inspire *Decision*. We do this by making it easier for people to:

- choose the important targets to pursue
- commit to pursuing them
- achieve them in addition to their everyday operational work.

Three mindsets help us achieve this, as we inspire our organisation to practise the organisational habit of *Decision:*

1. *Cascade, don't fragment.* Create a line of sight for every team to the corporate direction and delegate authority to improve.

2. *Buy-in, not sign-off.* Communicate the corporate direction in a way that engages everyone.

3. *Work on, not just in.* Give the authority (priority, time and resources) to work on the business and not just in it.

The starting point is to cascade strategy throughout the organisation, so everyone can see their part in it. As discussed in chapter 5, making the strategy broad and vague is *not* the way to achieve this! We need a different mindset about how to cascade strategy, so when we inspire the organisational habit of *Decision*, we are creating a line of sight for every team to the corporate direction and delegating authority to improve what matters.

Cascade, don't fragment

If safety, customer loyalty, cost reduction and innovation are important performance areas for the organisation, does that mean they are important for *everyone* in the organisation? Should every business unit and team and personal scorecard be a 'mini-me' version of the corporate scorecard?

Let's consider safety. If reducing lost-time injuries is a corporate goal, imagine what it would be like if everyone had to measure lost-time injuries. What sense would that make? Does everyone in the organisation have the same impact on or exposure to lost-time injuries? Is it the best use of everyone's time to work to improve safety? Of course not. What would the marketing team focus on if their scorecard wasn't cluttered with KPIs related to every corporate goal? They'd probably focus on what they exist to create, which is a growing number of leads that match the organisation's ideal market and are interested in the organisation's products. It's much more valuable for them to measure this than to measure how many paper cuts and stapler mishaps should be classified as lost-time injuries. This approach of 'mini-me' cascading of corporate strategy is used because it's simple, and requires no deliberate decision on the part of each business unit or team or individual. But it doesn't achieve meaningful goals throughout the organisation.

The principles of cascading

Cascading requires four basic principles, and we get the best of both worlds: we make sure that what gets measured at the team level is meaningful to the team, at the same time as having a strong line of sight to corporate goals.

Principle 1: Cascade by building the cause–effect chain, not by duplication

If a corporate goal is about customers that are more loyal, then we'd ask 'What makes customers loyal?' to determine the first level of cascading. We might end up with things such as:

- attracting more ideal customers
- keeping promises to customers
- solving customers' real problems.

We'd cascade these to the next level (say, teams), by asking 'What makes it possible to attract more ideal customers?' We'd keep this line of questioning until we reached individuals and their contribution to the cause–effect chain. The goals of any business unit, team or individual become both directly related to the work they do and aligned to corporate priorities.

Principle 2: Only cascade to where there is highest leverage

Only a few parts of the organisation will truly have a worthwhile impact on a corporate goal. Operations generally has the biggest impact on safety and timely delivery, for example. Marketing generally has the biggest impact on which customers we attract. As we cascade our strategy, we must keep asking 'Where is the biggest leverage?' Fracturing everyone's focus across all strategic goals they *could* impact will ensure they can't give their all to the one or two goals they *should*.

Principle 3: Build a map of the organisation's strategy

Maintaining links between all the goals that are chosen, from top to bottom in our organisation, will make it easier to test the logic of cause–effect, and to communicate throughout the organisation what matters and why. Maps bring everything together, so we can all see the whole, and navigate to find where we are in it. And we can start seeing something more than the cascading — we can see the collaboration between and among business units and teams. Strategy does not have to be force-fit into silos.

> Strategy does not have to be force-fit into silos.

Principle 4: Involve everyone in the process of determining their line of sight to corporate goals

We find the most meaning in things we take part in discovering and creating. People throughout our organisation will not only have the best idea of how they contribute to company goals, but their buy-in will be deep and true if they take part in the cascading process. They

We need buy-in, for without it not much will change.

are the ones to ask those questions described in principle 1. We need buy-in, for without it not much will change.

All leaders want goals and measures and activities to be aligned to the strategic direction. Leadership is, after all, about aligning people to a shared purpose. Alignment means that goals and measures and activities throughout an organisation sensibly and usefully relate to one another. These relationships make it possible for everyone to see how they contribute to the organisation. And seeing is believing.

Results Maps

Strategy maps, developed by the authors of *The Balanced Scorecard*, are the most commonly used visual representation of strategy on a single page. They:

- give us a succinct, big-picture snapshot of how pieces of the corporate strategy fit together
- highlight the cause–effect relationships among those pieces
- make it easier for leaders to describe the strategy to others.

But there are a few limitations:

- Usually these strategy maps are constructed in tiers. There will be the corporate tier. Then more tiers are created as the strategy is cascaded, so each area has its own strategy map. But it's hard to immediately see the linkages between the tiers.
- The strategy is often cascaded by structure, rather than by business process. So it's harder to find the root causes to design strategy execution around.
- The linkages in strategy maps are almost always cause–effect only. But there are certainly other important relationships between goals, such as conflict relationships where one goal might limit or sabotage another, or companion relationships where two goals work synergistically together.
- The strategic objectives in strategy maps are almost always written with weasel words.

Another type of map does what the strategy map does, and also overcomes these limitations. It's called a Results Map, an example of which is shown in figure 8.1, illustrating the cause–effect flow of results for two processes through to one of the ultimate results for a fire department. The Results Map is one of the PuMP techniques. Goals are placed in zones arranged in concentric circles. These zones are aligned to levels of decision making, from corporate to process owner and from process owner to in-process teams. And each goal is linked to the others it has a strong relationship with, whether it's cause–effect, conflict or companion.

Figure 8.1: a fire department's Results Map

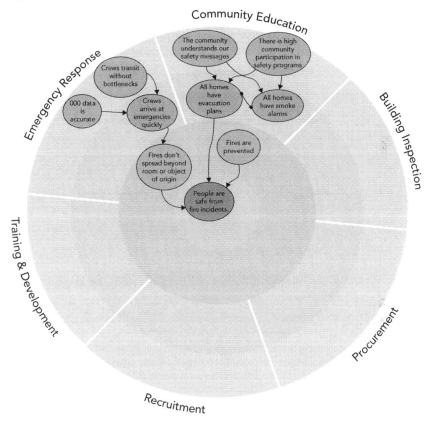

Results Map zones

The zones in a Results Maps make cascading and aligning strategy easier. There are almost always four zones in a Results Map:

1. The centre zone is for the results of our organisation's mission and vision.
2. The second zone from the centre is for the results of our strategic plan.
3. The third zone from the centre is for the results of departmental or customer-facing business process outcomes.
4. The outermost zone is for the results of teams or business units or sub-processes.

These zones are arranged so we can see how strategy cascades outward from the centre, and how people can see alignment from their work through to the organisation's purpose.

Results Map bubbles

The bubbles in a Results Map are measurable performance results. They are the product of practising the first evidence-based leadership habit of *Direction*. There is no place for actions on a Results Map. If we try to measure things such as 'train staff in negotiation', we'll just end up with a silly and trivial measure such as 'number of staff trained'.

And there is no place for weasel words on a Results Map. If we try to measure something such as 'enhance innovation', we'll end up with an uninformative measure such as 'number of new ideas generated'. Bleh. And people won't understand it specifically enough to find their best contribution. Rather, each bubble on a Results Map contains a unique performance result that is expressed as though it were a fact, and in measurable language, such as these:

- Customers are loyal.
- Products are delivered at the time the customer was promised.
- Employees are not harmed at work.

The performance results in the Results Map are linked to one another. These links show how the cause–effect contributions line up, from the results owned by teams all the way up to the

corporate results. We can see this in figure 8.1 (p. 111) for the Community Education team.

Putting it into everyday language, their line of sight to the strategic direction would read like this: As the team improves how well its safety messages are understood by the community, more of the community will be 'fire smart'. Then as that increases, more homes will have evacuation plans, and more homes will have smoke alarms. When these increase, more fires will be prevented, and ultimately this will mean less injury and loss from fire incidents.

Results Map relationships

The relationships in a Results Map tell a richer story than just cause–effect, which we generally use to draw a line of sight. There are four relationship types on a Results Map:

1. *Cause–effect.* By achieving one result, the other is more likely to be achieved.
2. *Companion.* Both results are synergistic and need to be achieved together.
3. *Conflict.* Achieving one result puts the other result at a high risk of being sabotaged.
4. *Lead–lag.* A special type of cause-effect relationship where there is a time delay — and therefore predictive power — between the lead and the lag result.

Strategy is often not linear, and the Results Map allows us to tell the story of strategy more flexibly. And, as we practise the habit of *Evidence*, each of these performance results will be measured, and the measures can be added to the Results Map to add more focus to the story of the strategy.

Decision: They want to work for something bigger than themselves

113

Where's Wally?

The CEO of one of the first organisations to use Results Mapping nicknamed the Results Map the *'Where's Wally* Diagram' (you might know it as *'Where's Waldo'*). The nickname was for two reasons. Firstly, it was because the Results Map is, admittedly, quite a busy diagram at first glance. Not quite as challenging as looking at a *Where's Wally* cartoon, though. And you can successfully explain it in just a couple of minutes. Secondly, and mainly, it was because once Wally is found in the map, Wally knows where he fits in the organisation. Wally has a line of sight from his work results through to the organisation's priorities and purpose. Seeing that line of sight in a single diagram is one of the most powerful uses of a Results Map, and time and again it makes it so easy for people to take that *Decision* — to focus on what matters most.

The Results Map also makes it much easier, when we cascade strategy, to draw logical cause–effect chains that align the organisation's parts to that strategy. There are two ways we can build this alignment when we cascade corporate direction and help Wally find himself.

A good way and a great way to cascade corporate strategy

Cascading a strategy requires a framework to break the strategy down into the unique contributions of each part and level of the organisation. We'll explore two frameworks:

1. The most common method is to cascade through the organisation's functional structure.
2. The less-known and more powerful way is to cascade through the organisation's business processes.

Cascade strategy through the organisation's structure

Organisational structure is the way that domains of responsibility are divided up. This is usually done through:

- departments
- divisions

- business units
- teams.

There are many names for these parts of structure, and they are used differently in different organisations. Each part of the structure is headed up by an executive, manager, supervisor or team leader. Cascading strategy through the organisation's structure is common, mostly because:

- it's convenient
- it's easy to understand
- the command chain is clear
- alignment to budgeting is simpler.

The way that strategy is cascaded through the organisation's structure is a bit like this:

- Each of the highest level of structure (such as a department) examines the impact they have on the strategic goals, and they set departmental goals.
- Each division within each department examines the departmental goals, and they set divisional goals.
- Each business unit within each division examines the divisional goals, and they set business unit goals.
- Each team within each business unit examines the business unit goals, and they set team goals.
- Each person within each team examines the team goals, and they set individual goals.

Take the example of a construction company that designs and builds family homes. They have five departments: Sales & Marketing, Finance & HR, Contracting & Design, Projects, and Purchasing. Imagine the company defines its success by two results: 'Predictably increasing returns for shareholders' and 'Customers fall in love with their new home'. And imagine that it has a strategic goal of 'New home throughput increases'. A typical structural cascade of a strategic goal such as this might be as follows:

1. Sales & Marketing examines the strategic goal, and sets themselves a goal of 'New home sales keep us booked a year in advance'.

2. Marketing examines this goal and sets themselves the goal of 'New home enquiries are regular and frequent'.

3. Outreach examines Marketing's goal, and sets themselves the goal of 'Advertising reaches a wider audience'.

This certainly makes it clear which team or level in the organisation is responsible for which goals. And it's clear how each team contributes to the corporate direction. But there are some downsides of structural cascading.

The first downside is that it ignores the white space — the handover points across structural boundaries, between:

- teams
- business units
- divisions
- departments.

The risk here is that Sales & Marketing could create more demand than Contracting & Design can handle, and the reputation of the company could be damaged. Or, worse, lower-quality designs could be handed over to Projects to build.

The second downside of structural cascading is that the cause–effect chain that links team goals through to strategic goals can be too weak. For example, Sales & Marketing and its teams may be better off focusing on the *quality* of the new home enquiries they generate, rather than the quantity. It might be more important for the reputation of the company that they attract better home projects, not more of them.

A third downside of structural cascading is that more change than necessary can occur, where everyone across the organisation is trying to improve at least one thing that relates to each strategic goal. More likely, though, is that just one or two areas are the real bottlenecks getting in the way of better performance and all the change energy should go to those. Everyone else either helps with the bottlenecks, or gets on with their business as usual.

Cascade strategy through the organisation's processes

Business processes are the flow of tasks and activities, in logical and sequenced order, that deliver services to customers. They are cross-functional, in that they flow across and between and through myriads of departments, divisions, business units and teams. Process cascading is great at avoiding white space problems and internal competition. The cause–effect chains are stronger because it's easier to find root causes or bottlenecks holding performance back. And the customer is always in focus. Strategy can be cascaded through the organisation's business processes through these three steps:

1. The main cross-functional core processes of the organisation are identified and mapped.

2. Each process team examines the strategic goals, and they set process outcome goals.

3. Each sub-process team within each core process examines the process outcome goals, and they set sub-process goals.

Let's return to the construction company's strategic goal of 'New home throughput increases'. Now, look at how strategy could be cascaded through the core process of the end-to-end client experience:

1. The process outcome goal might be 'Build cycle time decreases.'

2. The process flowchart is analysed to find where the bottlenecks or weak links are. Perhaps they find two sub-processes that have bottlenecks: the design approval sub-process has too much rework that holds up contracting, and the procurement sub-process has too many delays.

3. The design approval sub-process examines the process outcome goal, and sets the goal of 'Designs are correct each time'.

4. The procurement sub-process examines the process outcome goal, and sets the goal of 'Materials are delivered in full and on time'.

5. In turn, Sales & Marketing would notice that the rework in the design approval sub-process is because they are converting the wrong new home enquiries into sales, focusing too much on the easy conversions and not enough on the customers that are clear about what they want. So they set a goal of 'The clients we attract know what they want'.

Process cascading is great, but of course not without its downsides. The biggest downside is that few organisations have a business process model, and it is a big effort to build one. The learning curve to build it (properly) as we cascade our strategy can be too overwhelming. Secondly, there isn't usually one right answer to what an organisation's process model should look like. So people can be frustrated and worried that haven't got it right. But process cascading is ultimately superior. Here's why:

- It removes internal competition over resources, because resources are seen now in the context of end-to-end processes.

- It reduces duplication or wasted effort that comes from everyone trying to fix something, without really knowing if it's worth fixing.

- It finds where the greatest leverage for improvement lies, and that means the right resources can be given to the right team to fix the biggest bottlenecks that hold performance back.

- The very act of analysing processes to find what the important improvement goals are makes finding the right improvement initiatives faster and easier.

- Most importantly, process cascading takes the spotlight off people as the lowest common denominator of organisational performance, and throws that spotlight onto process design. This sets a climate where blame is removed, and collaboration, creativity, and continual learning and improvement can flourish.

This final point is critically important in inspiring *Decision* as an organisational habit. It makes it possible for people to truly buy in and contribute to achieving what's corporately important. The distinction between buy-in and sign-off is the next mindset for how we inspire the organisational habit of *Decision*, and it's about how we communicate the corporate direction in a way that engages everyone.

CASCADE, DON'T FRAGMENT

When we cascade strategy, we draw logical cause–effect chains that align the organisation's parts to that strategy. Each team has a line of sight from the results they own, to the results of the organisation as a whole.

Buy-in, not sign-off

Buy-in is a state where people are:

- committed to something
- convinced of its worth
- free of objections or fears.

It's when they feel they own something, or at least part of it. They won't hesitate to give their time and energy and talent to it. They won't even mind if it's hard work. We want our managers and employees to feel this way about the performance of the organisation, but we don't realise that we might actually be getting in the way of buy-in naturally happening.

Performance measurement, as a cornerstone of organisational performance, has such a stigma. Many people associate it with the inane drudgery of data collection, with the embarrassment of being compared with whoever is performing best this month, with the unfairness of what feels like their whole person being judged according to a few trivial numbers. The emotions people typically feel for performance measurement are frustration, cynicism, defensiveness, anxiety, stress and — at the root of all these — fear.

What we really want is for performance measurement to be seen as a natural and essential part of work. We want people to associate it with:

- learning more about what works and what doesn't
- valuable feedback that keeps us on the right track
- continuous improvement of business success.

The emotions we want people to feel for performance measurement are curiosity, pride, confidence, anticipation, excitement and — at the root of all these — empowerment. How can we create this kind of buy-in?

Don't block the flow of buy-in

Buy-in is like an underground spring that wants to bubble up and flow forth. But most of what we do in cascading strategy and measuring it is akin to piling rocks over that natural spring, stopping its flow. The answer is that we don't have to create buy-in, we just have to *not* do things that block its flow.

The first thing not to do is dictate the team's goals. Instead, help teams explore and decide how they most affect the corporate goals. If they build their own line of sight from the activities they perform through to the ultimate success outcomes for the organisation, they will get a much deeper understanding of the corporate direction and feel a deeper sense of ownership of their part in it.

> Buy-in is like an underground spring that wants to bubble up and flow forth.

And for similar reasons, we also don't tell the team what to measure. Instead, we show them how to design measures that best prove their results. They are the experts in what they do and in understanding the results they produce. If they are handed a ready-made set of performance measures, they will likely feel such measures are trivial, too generic or just not quite right. And that will stop them from owning them. Plus, their understanding of their contribution to corporate direction will deepen through the process of designing their own measures.

Support the measures

We can't judge the team's measures, either. Judgement kills buy-in faster than almost anything. Rather, encourage the team to invite feedback from their broader network of stakeholders, to test and fine-tune their measures by seeking input. The team's customers, advisers, partners and other team members can each bring a different perspective to the relevance and feasibility of the measures, and their collective feedback will be unbiased and comprehensive. This communication brings the team closer to their stakeholders, helps them understand what their stakeholders need and can contribute, and breaks down those silos that inevitably happen when we draw organisational boundaries. And this, in turn, helps the team see beyond their tasks to the impact those tasks have, on both the organisation's success and their stakeholders' success.

While we don't judge the team's measures, we also shouldn't let them default to trivial measures that are easy or convenient or traditional. Instead encourage and support the team to bring the right measures to life, even if it means replacing existing measures or collecting new data. Encourage them to learn how to collect the data their measures need, and make careful decisions about which measures will be worth the effort to implement and which won't.

For a team to truly own a set of performance measures that will focus them on improving performance, those measures must be for their own use. We need to break down any assumptions that measures are for 'reporting upwards' by giving the team the space to:

- design how they will report their measures
- choose the types of supplementary information they need for cause analysis
- interpret and respond to their own measures.

Just as we do at the strategic level for the organisation, teams need to continually learn how they can:

- improve their outcomes
- find the constraints on achieving those outcomes
- test the points of highest leverage to remove those constraints.

The most useful conversations we can have with teams are about their conclusions about the performance of their processes, and the impact of their targets and improvement ideas on corporate goals.

Buy-in is a natural product of respecting that people are wired to do a good job, to contribute their talents and efforts, and to make a positive difference. The evidence-based leader is more a mentor than a manager, showing how to engage in the performance of the organisation by practising at the strategic level the behaviours we want to see at all other levels. The idea is to make it safe for people to take charge not just of working in the business, but working on it, too.

> Buy-in is a natural product of respecting that people are wired to do a good job, to contribute their talents and efforts, and to make a positive difference.

As buy-in for measuring and improving performance grows, the high-performance culture grows too:

- Performance starts improving, even before improvement initiatives are implemented, because daily attention is more firmly fixed on what matters.
- People have more energy and enthusiasm because they are coming to work for a higher meaning. They have discovered something more motivating than the tasks they do: the impact their work has on others.
- Improvement happens faster, as people focus on what matters and on the proper analysis that reveals the root causes and points of highest leverage.

- Boundaries between organisational units start blurring, as more conversation and collaboration happens around the handover points in cross-functional business processes.
- Blame is replaced by curiosity, cause analysis and collaboration.

Fundamental to a high-performance culture is that people practise performance measurement and improvement as part of their 'real work'. They routinely spend time not just getting the job done, but also working on their *processes* to get the job done better. This is our next mindset for inspiring everyone to practise the organisational habit of *Decision*.

BUY-IN, NOT SIGN-OFF

We don't have to create buy-in; we just have to not do things that block its flow. Stop telling teams what their goals and measures should be and give them the space and authority to create these themselves.

Work on, not just in

Working in our business processes means following the steps of that process to get the job done. But working *on* our business processes means taking time out to examine and improve the steps of the process so that the job can be done better.

We need to do both. If we work *in* our processes without ever working *on* them, the constant change of the business world will ensure the results we produce today will be different tomorrow. We'll go backwards, when we thought we were maintaining our position.

When we give people quotas or targets to hit each day or week or month, and check on their success each day or week or month, we'll drive them to push harder while working *in* their processes. Every day they'll turn up at work and skip lunch to make that extra sale. Or they'll cut corners to reduce the materials they use and save a few more dollars. Each day they'll just keep trying, by working faster or spending less time on things, or skipping steps they think might not really matter. The demand for them to keep hitting the numbers spares them no time to even notice the consequences of their efforts, or the constraints that limit their success. The treadmill is simply running faster. And they will, in time, have to step off for a breather, or get spat out the back.

This doesn't work because there is no leverage. It's all about more effort, and effort is like fuel — it will run out and performance will drop. Leverage comes only by working *on* the processes, so we can see the constraints on our performance. Constraints take many forms:

- The sales script that no longer speaks to the struggles customers really have these days.
- The lack of an easy-to-search database of solutions to the trickier help desk queries.
- The poorly written work procedure that confuses people into making mistakes.

The FAA, discussed in chapter 7, was wasting millions in lost productivity every year by taking months to find appropriate jobs for employees that failed the flight controller's exam. They discovered that the biggest constraint was the policy that required managers to approve transfers. This was the bottleneck. Only by taking the time to flowchart the transfer process, and see how it really worked, did they realise this. And within weeks the constraint was removed and the time to transfer 'training failures' was reduced by two-thirds.

When we work *on* our processes, to find and remove the constraints that hold performance back, we exercise leverage. We're doing the modern-day version of inventing the wheel. We create the wheel and no longer have to keep pouring in effort, day in and day out, to keep performance lifted. We set it and forget it, because our wheel has taken away the need for that effort.

At least until we decide that performance needs to be even better.

WORK ON, NOT JUST IN

Working on our business processes means taking time out to examine and improve the design of the process steps so that the job can be done better.

Decision in evidence-based leadership is about everyone owning their contribution to the organisation's purpose and direction. When people have the *Direction* from us, and the know-how and authority to choose the improvements they will focus on to contribute to the organisation's success, they're ready to make it happen. They're ready for the organisational habit of *Action*.

Decision: They want to work for something bigger than themselves

CHAPTER 9

ACTION: REACHING FOR INTRINSICALLY REWARDING TARGETS

Targets are funny things. They scare the living daylights out of some people, but motivate and compel others. Sometimes they are ignored, sometimes they are moved, sometimes they are taken too literally. A target can improve one result while simultaneously sabotaging another. There are people who can't do without them, and people who refuse to accept that they are good for anything at all.

But targets can play a very important role in performance management — when they're set up properly. They help us make the improvement we're seeking real and tangible. It's one thing to say that we want to reduce the waste our organisation sends to landfill. But it makes it so much more tangible to say we want to halve the amount of waste we send to landfill by the end of the year.

Targets quantify how far away we are from where we want to be, helping us appreciate the size of the performance gaps we need to close. We must be deliberate in deciding how we're going to close them — be confident our investment in closing those gaps will be worth it.

This chapter discusses the organisational habit of *Action* and the three mindsets that foster it, but a major component of understanding *Action* is targets. Targets give performance improvement a direction and a distance to reach for. And so targets, when they're designed and chosen well and couched in the context of continuous performance improvement, give *Action* a very deliberate focus: to close performance gaps. So first, let's discuss how to design and choose helpful targets, before we look into the mindsets that will put them to their highest use.

Action means closing performance gaps

Evidence-based leaders want to inspire action that closes performance gaps — action that changes how the organisation works, so that after that change performance is better, and stays better. Action that shifts as-is performance to match our targeted to-be performance. *Action* isn't about completing project milestones on time, or making sure all the budget is spent, or working harder *in* the process. *Action* means finding and removing the constraints that hold performance back. When the shackles of an outdated policy or redundant procedure or ambiguous instruction are removed, performance is liberated from that day forward, with no continuing effort.

The trouble with closing performance gaps is that we don't know exactly what's going to work. Not until we look, and try. We don't know what exactly it will take to close a specific performance gap at the time we set the target that defines that gap. To inspire a high-performance culture that closes performance gaps, there are two things about reaching targets that we need to reframe.

What do targets mean?

The first is to reframe what a target means. Too often, we talk about hitting targets or meeting quotas. And it feels like failure if we try, but miss. If we reframe it as *reaching* for targets, the energy changes. Now it feels like any forward progress is a success, because it's a journey of striving and learning and correcting and trying again. *Hitting* targets smacks of judgement and winning or losing. *Reaching for* targets is about learning to win.

Mining companies don't just dig big holes anywhere. They have discovery teams, elite geological engineers who look for and scope and evaluate many candidate sites for mineral deposits that are worth mining. I consulted with one such discovery team that had been given a target of one new discovery per year. They resented that target.

It's not hard to appreciate why. Even though there is science to locating worthwhile mineral deposits, there is some element of chance as well. You just can't know for sure the value of a site until it's mined. An absolute target of one discovery per year assumes that chance plays an insignificant role. To hit a target like this, the discovery team might recommend more of their candidate sites for mining, regardless of their quality, in the hope at least one of them would be a successful discovery. Or they might take shortcuts in scoping and evaluating steps to fit in more exploration, spreading themselves thinner. Both approaches are essentially building waste into the discovery process, making it cost more and, while the target might be hit, the longer-term return on investment would be sabotaged.

> Hitting targets smacks of judgement and winning or losing. Reaching for targets is about learning to win.

But if they instead focused on *reaching* for targets, rather than hitting them, the energy shifts. They'd be reaching for more discoveries worth mining. They'd want to reduce the time it took to find new discoveries. Instead of asking 'How can we hit the target of one discovery per year?' they'd be asking 'How can we reduce the time it takes to find new discoveries?' The energy shifts from trying harder, to finding leverage. The discovery team would take a closer look at their exploration process, searching for steps that could be done better or faster, or don't need to be done at all.

Who is accountable for targets?

The second thing to reframe about targets is their relationship to accountability. Usually, accountability means that someone will have to answer for a target being missed. And it feels like being blamed for something you can't really control (which is true; no one person can control if a target is hit or not). If we reframe accountability as monitoring performance, interpreting it validly and initiating action when needed (as defined in chapter 6), the threat goes away. Now it feels like we have the space to learn and discover, experiment and test, and master the skill of continuous performance improvement.

The mining company's discovery team were quite anxious about being held accountable for the target of one discovery per year. Not hitting that target would make them look incompetent or like they weren't trying hard enough. The team's leader would have to answer for the failure, at best missing out on a bonus and at worst losing their job. Hardly motivating. And completely unhelpful — after all, the constraints holding performance back are in the design of business processes, and virtually never in the people.

What the discovery team needs is encouragement to own their discovery process, and learn how to make it work better. If they are accountable for learning about what works best to reduce the time it takes to produce a discovery, they are accountable for what is within their control or influence. That's more motivating, and it also means performance will improve sooner — and without sabotaging other areas of performance.

Evidence-based leaders inspire *Action* by encouraging people to reach for targets, rather than hit them. They know that finding leverage is an unknown quantity. It's like running a series of experiments. Reaching for targets means encouraging running experiments to find out what gives the best leverage in closing performance gaps — and holding people accountable for this rather than hitting numbers.

Targets must be believed to be seen

What's your organisation's track record in reaching targets? Are the majority of targets reached within their set time frames, or is it more common to hear rationalisations as to why the majority of targets were not met? If it's the latter, it might be because your target setting process is a little too much about numbers and not nearly enough about emotion, about how people *feel* about the various aspects of target setting, pursuing and achieving. Here are some tips for setting targets that people will feel compelled to reach for, and therefore be more likely to achieve.

Tip 1: Targets must speak to the heart, not just the head

Targets that are an almost mathematical arrangement of 'performance measure + target value + time frame' speak loudly and clearly to the head. But they say nothing to the heart. What makes a target speak to the heart is rich and sensual language that tells vivid and compelling stories of the future as if the target had already been achieved.

This isn't magic. It's just our brain's RAS (reticular activating system), which is the part of the brain that decides what we give conscious attention to. Whatever turns our RAS on is what our mind will obsess over. If we've got our RAS turned on to drinking eight glasses of crystal-clear, cool, cleansing water every day, then something changes. Our mind makes us notice water coolers when we walk past them, notice how many other people have glasses of water on their desks or in their hands, and how dry and parched and desperate our mouth is for a sip.

Targets that stick to the old formula of 'performance measure + target value + time frame' evoke feelings of boredom, cynicism and pessimism. These are the emotions that:

- do not fuel action toward the target
- lead to misinterpretation of the target
- cause wasted effort pursing the wrong results
- allow other areas of performance to be sabotaged without regard.

Targets that are told with vivid and sensual stories are targets than unleash emotions such as anticipation, curiosity, excitement, desperation, impatience, passion and want. These are the emotions that move people toward targets (like yours truly toward chocolate).

Tip 2: Targets must live inside people's circle of influence

W. Edwards Deming says in his classic book *The New Economics:*

> How could there be life without aims and hopes? Everyone has aims, hopes, plans. But a goal that lies beyond the means of its accomplishment will lead to discouragement, frustration, demoralization. In other words, there must be a method to achieve an aim.

It's funny, but beliefs are often more real to people than facts. It takes some very strong experiences and immersion in facts to shift our long-held beliefs. Our beliefs, not data, drive our choices and behaviours. What we *believe* about the achievability of a target will drive how we feel about pursuing it more than the fact that it is written in our business plan.

Our beliefs, not data, drive our choices and behaviours.

Targets without any strategies or means for being achieved are targets that easily stimulate emotions of fear of failure, frustration, procrastination and confusion. Such emotions quash the motivation (if it ever existed) and intention of reaching the target. Early action is important to build and keep the momentum of progress. Otherwise, figures are fudged, excuses are used to justify lack of progress and problems are swept under the rug.

Targets that are iteratively designed with preliminary ideas about how to achieve them and a realistic allocation of resources are more likely to stimulate emotions of trust, confidence, faith, curiosity and inquisitiveness. These emotions fuel action, and no worthy target can be achieved without action.

Tip 3: Targets must be owned to be pursued

People must see themselves in the endeavours they pursue, or they won't put themselves into those endeavours. Targets imposed from on high, set without the involvement of those that will pursue them, are targets doomed to fail. It's certainly important for people to work for the good of the organisation, but this can only happen if the organisation can work for the good of the people.

Targets that aren't owned by the people responsible for achieving them lead to:

- fear of being blamed for results outside their control
- stress from feeling pulled away from personal priorities
- anger
- resentment
- humiliation.

These emotions disempower people, and disempowered people can't perform. Little or no productive action happens to achieve the target.

When someone can see a personal benefit in pursuing a target for the organisation, there's hope. Knowing the personal values of individuals helps most here; it makes it easier to match people to targets, and to refine and tailor targets to accommodate people's personal goals along the way. This way, the emotions of pride, high self-esteem, passion, dignity and commitment flourish, and they turbo-charge the progress toward target.

***

Reaching targets is fundamental to the organisational habit of *Action*. And the three mindsets that will increase the chances of closing those performance gaps and reaching important targets are:

1. *Causes, not symptoms.* Find ways to remove the constraints that limit capability and not compensate for lack of capability.
2. *Practical, not perfect.* Build the momentum of performance improvement by progressing when it's 80 per cent perfect, rather than waiting for 100 per cent.
3. *Collaboration, not competition.* Find and fix the problems that exist in the white space on the organisational chart: the handover points between business units, functions and teams.

Causes, not symptoms

We have a culture of treating symptoms. When we have a headache, more of us will reach for the paracetamol than for a tall glass of water. When we have a hormone imbalance, we're more likely to undergo hormone replacement therapy than remove hormone disruptors from our environment and diet.

In business, the symptom-treating culture thrives. When we ask the development approvals team to double the approvals they process, they will say they need to double the number of staff and likely not even consider that there is wasted time in their approvals process. Should we wish to fill empty positions faster, the recruitment team might suggest that HR executives need to be reminded more often to sign off approvals more quickly and not think to question the need for HR executive approval on every new recruit.

We're good at treating symptoms, but symptoms return as soon as we back the treatment off. In business, the treatment is often more of something: more people, more hours, more money, more expectations. This isn't improving performance; it's compensating for lack of performance.

> We're good at treating symptoms, but symptoms return as soon as we back the treatment off.

When we have a performance gap to close, we're better off looking for leverage: creating a fundamental performance improvement, rather than working harder to keep holding performance up.

Imagine a help desk team within the information services division in an organisation. Their manager copped an earful at the monthly management meeting about help desk wait times. So the manager declares to the team to do whatever it takes to resolve problems faster. In fact, they are now given the target of resolving 95 per cent of problems within 24 hours. *That should motivate them*, thinks the manager.

What do they do? How do they improve performance to reach that target? At first, they feed off motivation and work faster for a while.

When the motivation wears off, they work into their breaks and after hours. When they can't add any more work hours, they start to cut corners, and 'forget' to capture the harder problems in the help desk system, or close off unsolved problems if the 24-hour window isn't met. This is not fundamental performance improvement. This is compensating for a business process that is incapable of delivering the level of performance asked of it.

Now imagine, instead, that the manager and the help desk team together flowcharted the problem resolution process, capturing the way it currently happens. And imagine that the team looked at that as-is flowchart and talked about where it takes too long, and why. Perhaps they see that finding solutions takes a long time because they're not sharing fixes and solutions with each other. Or perhaps they see for the first time just how much red tape there is. They are discovering the constraints that are keeping resolution time from being faster.

Imagine that they decide to redesign their problem resolution process, to share fixes and solutions with each other, to remove red tape and to standardise the fastest diagnostic technique. Suddenly, they are resolving problems quicker and catching up on the unresolved backlog. They're not working any harder — in fact it feels easier. Their resolution accuracy is better. Their customers stop complaining. That's a fundamental performance improvement: a one-time change that elevates all future performance without any further effort.

The only thing that stops most people, in my observation, from making fundamental performance improvements, is excuses.

Not enough staff is an excuse, not a reason

As excited as they might be about having meaningful performance measures that they chose themselves, and that clearly link to their goals, when it comes to setting improvement targets, the most common retort from people is, 'Yeah, but we don't have enough staff to make that happen!'

What they are really saying is, 'The number of staff we have is the primary cause of how good our results are.' They don't know they're saying this. It's just that they've never drawn a distinction between working harder *in* the business and working smarter *on* the business. The whirlwind of working *in* their processes blinds them to the design flaws in those processes. 'This is how things are done around here,' they'll say. 'We've always done it this way.' They don't think to stop and sharpen the saw; they just get more people to help with the cutting.

There are times when some changes or improvements can't be made without more staff, particularly large and sudden increases in workload. For example, the growth of demand from customers as a result of a wildly successful marketing campaign that the delivery team didn't expect, or a sudden doubling of projects resulting from a merger of departments. Sometimes we do need more staff, but these are extenuating circumstances, or special and rare cases. But more often than not, adding more staff is just compensating for a process that isn't capable enough. And compensating for performance is not leverage.

As Albert Einstein said, we can't solve a problem with the same level of thinking that created the problem. We need a level of thinking that helps us find the root causes that are choking our processes so they can't perform any better.

The performance measure is the lens

Too many improvement projects start with great intentions to make a process better, but they should start with something else: a measure. The reason we invest time and money into improvement projects is because we have a goal that's not been achieved yet. And any goal worth achieving will have a measure, and a target. The measure will show us that there is an unacceptable gap between as-is performance and to-be performance, and our improvement project should

> Any goal worth achieving will have a measure, and a target.

close as much of that gap as possible. The measure needs to be the lens through which we search for causes that constrain performance.

Naturally, when we find the causes that are holding open that gap between as-is performance and to-be performance, we want to be rid of them. And as we try and do that, we must be careful not to fall into the perfection trap. The next mindset of inspiring the organisational habit of *Action* is about how we can prevent the loss of momentum due to perfectionism.

CAUSES, NOT SYMPTOMS

Fight the culture of fire-fighting. Stop wasting time and resources on solutions that treat symptoms. The obvious solution is rarely the best. The best solutions to close performance gaps cure the causes.

Practical, not perfect

In 1897, an Italian economist named Vilfredo Pareto made the discovery that 80 per cent of the wealth of a population was owned by 20 per cent of its people. The Pareto Principle, or 80/20 rule, is a pattern of predictable imbalance that has since become part of business vernacular. The quality movement, throughout the middle of the last century, embraced the 80/20 rule as a guide for how to think about improving things: '80 per cent of the problem comes from 20 per cent of the causes.'

If we want a measure or a result to improve, we have to change something. And with even a basic 80/20 analysis, we can find out what those 'somethings' are that will have the greatest impact in improving that measure or result.

As evidence-based leaders, we're aiming for high-ROI strategy execution, and that means finding leverage. We want the organisation to think deliberately about which initiatives will have the most leverage to close performance gaps, to get a high ROI. But striving for perfection will never get a high ROI, because perfection requires too much time and effort. The more time and effort the more investment and, consequently, the lower the ROI.

But we still want excellence, and we can have it when we focus more on practicality than on perfection. So principles such as the 80/20 rule are ideal. They help us be deliberate about finding excellence leverage, rather than being dogmatic about finding perfect leverage.

Conducting an 80/20 analysis

A basic 80/20 analysis starts with questions like these:

- Which are the 20 per cent of tasks that generate 80 per cent of the output?
- Who are the 20 per cent of customers that generate 80 per cent of our profitability?
- What are the 20 per cent of products that generate 80 per cent of our profitability?
- What are the 20 per cent of interruptions that cause 80 per cent of our productivity problems?
- What are the 20 per cent of complaints that take up 80 per cent of our complaint handling time?

The 80/20 rule gives us a fast track to find the things that have the biggest likely impact on the results we want. And by focusing on those things, we can more quickly and easily examine how we can influence them, and start influencing them, often well before we'd get anywhere near to finding the 'perfect' solution.

The basic way to do a simple 80/20 analysis starts with framing the result and its potential causes in 80/20 questions such as those listed earlier. That sets the scope for what kind of data to collect. If we're going to know the 20 per cent of causes that produce 80 per cent of the result, we need to measure both the result and the degree of impact of each cause. If it's uncertain exactly what to collect data about, we can use a cause–effect diagram (also known as a fishbone diagram — see figure 9.1) to map out the possibilities. Then we can measure or estimate the relative impact of each cause on the end result.

Figure 9.1: fishbone diagram of constraints on customer loyalty

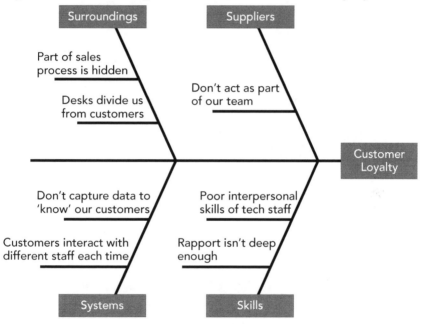

A simple bar chart or Pareto chart is a great way to display the 80/20 analysis once the data is collected. Each cause will have a number that represents the size of its impact on the result. It might be dollars or hours or incidents, depending on the result. Chart the data as per figure 9.2 (overleaf) and look for the tallest 20 per cent of bars in the chart that visually account for about 80 per cent of the measure.

Figure 9.2: Pareto chart of reasons that customers defect

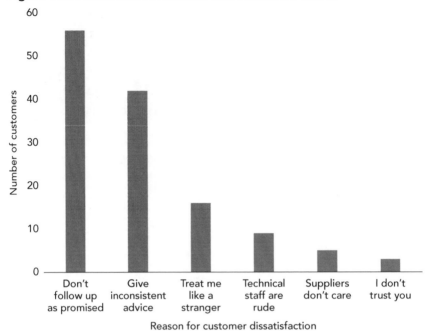

Of course, it won't always be 80/20. Sometimes the patterns will be 99/1, or 90/10 or 70/30. That's fine. The point is that cause–effect relationships are imbalanced; rarely will the pattern be that 50 per cent of the causes produce 50 per cent of the effect. So we prioritise, and give our attention to the 20 per cent that matters most right now. The 80/20 rule is not really a rule, and it's not the point. The point is that the easiest and quickest way to improve performance, to close those strategically important performance gaps, is to be practical. Being practical means taking action when there is just enough information to choose an action that will significantly improve performance.

When it's 80 per cent there, it's good enough

The Pareto Principle lends itself to another useful guideline for being practical in how we close performance gaps. It's the 80 per cent rule. The idea is that when something is 80 per cent good enough, it's time to move forward. Again, it won't be exactly 80 per cent. But there is a tipping point, a point past which any extra effort or time will only produce diminishing returns at best, and will reverse progress at worst. We know we're at that tipping point, or just past it, in fact, when we feel like we're spinning our wheels, our conversation is going around in circles and our momentum grinds to a halt.

Just as there is a risk of under-thinking our performance improvement approach by implementing solutions that are completely untested or unrelated to the root causes, there is also the risk of over-thinking it. We need to walk the boundary line between the two, and it's a subjective boundary. Regular reflection is the easiest way to keep close to that boundary line. First, we check:

1. Has our conversation circled back around to the same questions, the same comments, the same words?
2. Are we talking, but not making any decisions that move us forward to the next step in our approach?
3. Do we feel tired, bored, frustrated, or unhappy with where we are right now?

Then if any of these questions are answered 'yes', we consolidate:

1. Which causes and potential solutions have we agreed on so far?
2. Is there a direct link between the solutions and the causes?
3. If we implemented one of these solutions, what would we expect the impact on our result or measure to be?
4. Is that expected impact worthwhile enough to go ahead and test the solution?

The idea is to get movement, to find the next best action to take that will close the performance gap we're focused on. When we reach or pass the tipping point, whatever ideas we have are the ideas we should go with. We will learn through action now, because we've learned all we can from talking and thinking (without wasting too much time and energy).

And we won't sabotage our ROI if we are also practical in implementing the solution that is our next best action to close the performance gap. There are a few approaches that are known for their practicality, and one of the most interesting is Google Venture's design sprints.

Compress the time to find viable solutions

Design sprints are fast and focused business experiments that achieve in a week what many new initiatives, innovations and improvement projects take months to do. Created by Google Ventures and detailed in *Sprint*, a book authored by Jake Knapp, Braden Kowitz and John Zeratsky, design sprints are based on a rapid-fire version of the PDCA cycle (plan, do, check and act), and inspired by a few other approaches popular in software development, applied to a bounded problem or opportunity. The steps are:

1. Idea
2. Build
3. Launch
4. Learn

and they are implemented over a five-day schedule.

Even though they are more often associated with software development, they work in all kinds of small business and corporate contexts, such as education, sales, publishing, health and branding. There are over a hundred design sprints documented at www .sprintstories.com.

In the context of closing a performance gap, a design sprint is a great approach to focus on practicality and not be slowed down by the distraction of perfection. To roughly outline how a design sprint unfolds, here's how one education research company used the method to kick off their ambitions to increase graduation rates in the American education system with adaptive learning.

Monday

The team starts off by scoping the situation and context, defining the performance gap, and setting a realistic focus and target for the sprint. The performance gap they want to close is to increase the time that teachers spend coaching students in applying knowledge, and reduce the time teaching it. Their focus for the design sprint is to create a tool that will make it faster and easier to personalise lessons for each student.

Tuesday

Now the team explores existing and new solutions to close the performance gap, clearly articulates those potential solutions, and then defines and recruits the target customers to test with on Friday. The education research team realises that before a teacher can personalise a lesson for a student, they need to understand how that student's learning is going. So most of the potential solutions the team comes up with involve some kind of performance reporting for students.

Wednesday

On the third day of the design sprint, the team critiques each potential solution, chooses those that have the best chance of success, and maps out a storyboard of how they would work. The chosen solution for the tool to increase teachers' coaching-to-teaching ratio ends up blending a few elements of several potential solutions, but they realise it also needs to very quickly capture information about students' own learning goals and ways to quantify their progress.

Thursday

The team builds the potential solution so it can be tested as though it were real. Keynote and InVision (a prototyping app) are used to throw together a sample app for teachers to play with, that simulates the essential functions of setting student goals, designing student learning sessions and monitoring student performance.

Friday

The prototype solution is now tested with the recruited customers, and everyone observes what happens and assesses whether the solution worked or not. The prototype adaptive learning tool is tested with some teachers. The education research team learns that the personalised learning module is confusing, that the student goals and performance measures need better data, and that the reports really excite the teachers because they can help them adjust their teaching strategies before it's too late for the student.

In summary, the education research team didn't have the final solution, not by a long shot. But they had tested their hypothesis that this kind of reporting really could help teachers to personalise the learning experience for their students. And in a mere five days, the education research company had found a viable solution to continue investing in (likely with more design sprints).

Benefits of deliberate improvement

Design sprints are iterative, but they will close performance gaps faster because of the high cadence of learning and testing all the way through the length of the improvement initiative. A very practical guide to conducting design sprints can be found at www.gv.com/sprint/. This rapid-fire improvement approach lends itself to many performance improvement challenges we face in all sectors and industries. But it might not suit situations when performance gaps are more complex to understand, diagnose and close.

Even still, a deliberate improvement method will help us be as practical as we can in our pursuit for high-ROI improvement. Lean Six Sigma is a more conventional improvement method that has more structured steps than design sprints, and a very specific focus on reducing the waste and defects in business processes that hold open our performance gaps.

Focus on eliminating waste

The global success of business improvement methods such as Theory of Constraints, Lean Thinking, Six Sigma, and their subsequent blending, is largely due to their practical approach to improving

Rework is waste

When we have to:

- do something again because the first time didn't work
- make another one because the first one wasn't right
- correct a mistake

we're reworking. Rework is what happens when it's not right, first time. Example measures for rework include the:

- percentage of times it was right the first time
- total time spent fixing things
- percentage of total processing time that was rework time.

Redundancy is waste

If we're:

- doing tasks that don't need to be done at all
- stockpiling information or inventory just in case
- building in a lot of buffer time to allow for running late

we have redundancy. Some of the classic ways to measure redundancy are the:

- value of inventory items that are kept 'just in case' and don't directly contribute to goals or core business
- total time spent on tasks that don't contribute to goals or core business
- volume of data or information collected and captured that does not contribute to goals or core business.

Cycle time and reducing waste

Some leaders fantasise about the simplicity of having a single KPI that could drive excellence in their businesses. If such a fantastical KPI existed, it would likely be cycle time: the time it takes from when a customer or stakeholder declares a need for something to the time when they have that need fulfilled.

Measuring cycle time (and only in the context of fundamental performance improvement) is a very practical way to focus on waste reduction. Working to reduce the cycle time forces us to find and address where the different types of waste are in our processes. But as this happens, we find that other important outcomes are also consequently improved, including:

- customer satisfaction
- employee engagement
- cost reduction
- profit margins
- product quality
- service quality.

The reason is that the reduction of cycle time, through the elimination of waste, keeps the business design evolving so it better fulfils the organisation's purpose with the highest ROI possible. As the AGI-Goldratt Institute emphasises in its brilliantly titled book *Velocity* (a modernisation of the business classic *The Goal*), increasing operational speed in alignment with strategic direction is the fastest way to create high performance. Even in as little as a few months.

Collaborative approaches

In addition to their practicality, another feature that makes improvement approaches such as Lean Six Sigma, Theory of Constraints and design sprints so successful at closing performance gaps is that they are highly collaborative. They don't pit people against each other in the hope that a competitive atmosphere will drive everyone to perform better, and thus get the biggest performance improvement for the organisation. They don't assume that organisational performance is the sum of people's performance. As we've already explored, people's behaviour is rarely the root cause of performance gaps. Collaboration works so much better than competition at closing performance gaps.

Collaboration works so much better than competition at closing performance gaps.

The third mindset of inspiring the organisational habit of *Action*, and getting the right kind of collaboration, is about finding and fixing the problems that exist in the white space on the organisational chart: the handover points between business units, functions and teams.

> ## PRACTICAL, NOT PERFECT
>
> Give practicality a higher priority than perfection. Perfection paralyses progress. The fastest way to close performance gaps is to make practical decisions about the next best actions to take, and avoid the temptation of looking for the best solution first.

Collaboration, not competition

One of my most memorable experiences in facilitating a process improvement initiative was with a freight business that was struggling to get its customers to pay invoices on time. They were spending too much time chasing late payments in an effort to avoid bad debts. It would seem natural to assume that the invoicing team needed to fix something; no doubt they had asked for more resources to chase the late payments. And no doubt they had suggested that customers needed to be educated in how to read the invoices and pay them on time. Yet the problem persisted. Until a piece of information became available, serendipitously.

I was also helping the organisation to roll out a customer survey that would give each business unit a more practical analysis of customer satisfaction. They would use focus groups of customers to find out the top 10 attributes of service that mattered most to them when using that kind of service. These attributes of service would then form the basic questions of the survey, to quantify both their relative importance to customers and how satisfied customers were with each of them. Those attributes that had highest importance but lowest satisfaction would then become the focus of continuous improvement projects for the business units. The freight business found out from their first customer survey that one of the top three service attributes was, coincidentally, accuracy of invoices. Customers were not paying invoices because they were based on inaccurate or confusing rates. They didn't need education on how to read the invoices nor on how to pay invoices on time. They needed invoices that accurately matched the services they had purchased.

The organisation formed a cross-functional team to solve the problem, made up of invoicing staff, consignment officers and customer account managers. They began by defining three specific performance results: timely payment of invoices, revenue collected for all consignments handled, and ease of understanding of invoices. The process team then flowcharted the invoicing process. Nothing fancy, just lots of butcher's paper hung on a wall in a meeting room, sticky notes and coloured markers. But it was a revelation, something that they had never done before. It gave everyone their first view of the entire process, beyond their own part in it. They saw all the parts and, even more importantly, they saw the interactions among the parts.

When everyone agreed that their hand-drawn masterpiece was a fairly accurate description of how things actually happened in invoicing, they metaphorically walked through the flowchart again. With attention on both the parts and the interactions, they made notes of specific problems that affected invoice accuracy. These they called 'disconnects', where the process is disconnected from its purpose. They found three disconnects that stood out as the biggest problems affecting invoice accuracy:

1. Freight consignment notes were not always supplied when they should be, and freight was shipped without them. The team that received freight from the customer was focused on making sure the freight was shipped on time, and didn't give a thought to the link between consignment notes and the accuracy of invoicing. Invoicing wasn't their job, after all.

2. Freight consignment notes went missing when they were paper-based. The invoicing team would receive the shipment details either electronically or on paper consignment notes, and it depended on which freight depots were given the electronic consignment notes, and whether or not the electronic system worked on the day.

3. The wrong charges could be applied when the data about the exact type and amount of freight was not accurately provided by the customer. When customers turned up with freight that was different to what Receivals were told to expect, Receivals could hardly send the customer away, so they did their best to write down adjustments quickly and get the freight loaded and shipped, in full and on time.

Together, and without blame, the cross-functional freight team worked out the root causes of late invoice payments. Together, and without blame, they agreed how to fix them. And only by working together in this way could they ever have finally solved the problem. Time and again we realise this: that the root causes of our organisational performance problems are in the white space on the organisational chart, at the points where work is handed over from one team or business unit to another. No-one is managing — or even watching — the white space.

> The fastest and easiest way to stop the white space from behaving like a black hole is to encourage collaboration across those organisational boundaries.

Matrix organisation structures are one attempted solution to this problem. Employees report to both a functional manager and to a process or product line manager. But the fundamental problem of drawing lines and boundaries is still there. And so there is still white space. The fastest and easiest way to stop the white space from behaving like a black hole is to encourage collaboration across those organisational boundaries.

It starts with understanding the cross-functional business processes that produce the results we have decided to improve. Then it means designing our performance improvement projects to understand and analyse and change those cross-functional business processes. And the best way to execute those process improvement initiatives is through cross-functional teams, to get a thorough understanding of the process (and the problem) from end to end. To make this work, we need to stop pitting teams against one another. We need to replace competition with more collaboration.

Competition works for athletes, but not for organisations

We know that one of the most common uses of performance measures is to compare. Our logic is that if people and teams know their performance is being compared to others, then that should drive improved performance. In sport it works: competition is the greatest motivator for improving performance.

It might sound logical, but that's not what happens with organisational performance. In *Measurement Madness*, authors Dina Gray, Pietro Micheli and Andrey Pavlov share dozens of accounts of the dark side of using measurement for comparison in the hope of stimulating competition and performance improvement.

For example, in education, league tables rank schools based on examination pass rates. Because the rankings can influence parents' choices of which schools to send their children to, for schools to stay viable they need to be sure they only accept new students who have the ability to absorb and regurgitate knowledge (that is, to pass exams).

In health, hospitals that are measured and compared by patient survival rates will be less likely to admit high-risk patients. Due to the use of mortality rates of stroke victims to compare hospitals in the US, some hospitals were discharging patients early, so if they died at home they would not be counted in the hospital's mortality rates.

No organisation wants to be anywhere other than near the top of league tables, because their position (rightly or wrongly) affects the support they will get from customers and funders and the community. And that, of course, affects their future viability.

What good comes from comparing one organisation to others, or one CEO to others, or one team to others? The comparative measures only tell a part of the story. Hospitals that take on the most challenging patients may report high mortality rates, despite providing exceptional care and achieving relatively lower mortality rates for those

> Competition often drives dysfunctional behaviours.

challenging patients. Competition often drives dysfunctional behaviours to achieve the outcomes that are measured, not the outcomes that matter.

Wherever we draw boundaries and make comparisons, we create competition. Boundaries immediately establish an 'us vs them' mindset. We stay on our side; they stay on theirs. We do our bit, they do theirs. Comparison almost always escalates into defensiveness.

Within organisations, boundaries set up the same 'us vs them' dynamic. We talk about organisational silos or fiefdoms, and we observe the competition between them as each business unit vies for the resources and attention to maximise their performance. It might sound like a good thing: each team is forced to try harder and perform better. But it doesn't work, not in the long term. The resources and attention end up going to the teams that perform best at winning resources and attention. And that means the resources and attention aren't going to the teams that need them most, for the good of the whole organisation.

The whole is more than the sum of its parts

Organisations are wholes. Unlike machines, if they are pulled apart and put back together again, they won't be the same. They may not even survive the ordeal. Organisations are organisms: unlike machines, they are self-organising and adaptive. They can adapt, and even change, their environment. The parts of organisations are interdependent: one part can have a profound effect on the rest of the organisation. Peter Senge says it eloquently in his book *The Fifth Discipline*:

> Business and other human endeavours are also systems. They, too, are bound by invisible fabrics of interrelated actions, which often take years to fully play out their effects on each other. Since we are part of that lacework ourselves, it's doubly hard to see the whole pattern of change. Instead, we tend to focus on snapshots of isolated parts of the system, and wonder why our deepest problems never seem to get solved.

Senge is explaining systems thinking, and he is showing us that organisations are not the sum of parts; they are the interdependency and interplay of parts. So to change an organisation, to get better performance, we can't treat it like a machine. We can't unbolt a part of the organisation, change it, bolt it back in and expect it to perform better. Where and when the consequences and flow-on effects of any change in an organisation will be felt, and to what degree, are hard to predict. So it must be changed as a whole system. All improvement needs to be done with systems thinking, an appreciation of the interconnectedness and interdependency and dynamics that make the organisation a whole. Another systems thinking author, Donella Meadows, who is discussed in chapter 10, illustrates how easy it is to overlook interconnectedness:

> You think that because you understand 'one' that you must therefore understand 'two' because one and one make two. But you forget that you must also understand 'and'.

Systems thinking starts with bringing people together, people who have different perspectives and perceptions of the whole, so together they can build a richer and fuller understanding of the system, which is itself a part of an even bigger system. Whatever level of the system we're working in to create higher performance, collaboration ensures we treat that system like the organism it is, and allow it to learn.

Organisations are not the sum of parts; they are the interdependency and interplay of parts.

The next chapter is about how *Learning* can be inspired in evidence-based organisations.

COLLABORATION, NOT COMPETITION

The whole is more than the sum of its parts. To make high performance happen, we need to stop pitting teams against one another. We need to replace competition with more collaboration.

CHAPTER 10

LEARNING: SUCCESS LOVES SPEED

One of my all-time favourite books is *Zen and the Art of Motorcycle Maintenance* by Robert Pirsig. I mention it here because it pops up in a great book that gives insight into how evidence-based leaders should inspire learning in their organisations: *Thinking in Systems* by Donella Meadows. Discovering the following quote by Robert Pirsig at the start of Donella's book felt like serendipity, the convergence of the right ideas in the same time and place:

> If a factory is torn down but the rationality which produced it is left standing, then that rationality will simply produce another factory. If a revolution destroys a government, but the systematic patterns of thought that produced that government are left intact, then those patterns will repeat themselves ...

Learning means course correcting

If we fix our organisational performance problems with the same level of thinking that created them, the problems will simply resurface later. We stay stuck on the same course, even though on the surface we see lots of action and change. But whatever problems we think we're fixing now, we'll end up creating them again in some form.

A typical problem many organisations have is backlogs or queues, where unfinished work is waiting for the next step. They might be unresolved help desk problems, unfulfilled customer orders, overdue project tasks, or unspent budget close to the end of the financial year. A common way to think about backlog problems is that employees are not being productive enough. The solution is then a combination of:

- incentives to work harder
- education in time management
- clearer goals and targets
- more regular communication and coaching (which is sometimes really micromanagement).

The thinking that created this problem is that staff productivity determines how much gets done. And using this same level of thinking to solve the problem focuses on fixing staff productivity. But backlogs and queues have a tendency to grow, and not because productivity slackens off. (Which it's bound to do, incidentally, because the harder staff work to hit targets, the more burnt out they become. Resilience has its limits.)

To fundamentally solve the problem of backlogs and queues, once and for all, a different level of thinking is needed. We need to climb up a little higher to see the bigger picture, and the dynamic that's at play. The place where help desk problems are logged, and wait for attention, is merely one step in the problem resolution process. The next steps are:

1. allocating the problem to someone to fix it
2. analysis of the problem to look for the cause
3. fixing the assumed cause of the problem and seeing if the issue is resolved.

They might cycle back through the last two steps a few times, until the issue is finally resolved. The final step is letting the customer know it is resolved, and closing the case in the help desk system.

What we want is for help desk problems to flow smoothly through these steps, without getting stuck at any one of them. Rather than assume that staff are not productive enough in resolving problems quickly, a different level of thinking would have us looking for which steps are slowing down the flow. Which step is the bottleneck? And when we find that out, then we'd look at the design of that step to work out ways to open up the flow.

We've broadened our view of the system with the performance problem we want fixed. We've lifted our thinking to a higher level so we can see beyond our default solutions. And we find solutions that change the behaviour of the system and its capacity to flow. We learn something new about the system we manage.

Learning means course-correcting, changing not only the actions we take to solve performance problems, but also the way we think about solving problems. The foundation of this kind of learning is to treat change initiatives as experiments, to protect our learning from our assumptions as much as possible. Then we need to let the difficult learning (and shift in our mental models) happen, by opening ourselves to the lessons that only come from failure. We speed up the learning process, and therefore the changes that elevate organisational performance, by a series of iterations that help us fail fast and learn fast.

> Learning means course-correcting, changing … the way we think about solving problems.

This is the collection of mindsets that will make it easier for us to inspire the organisational habit of *Learning*:

1. *Experiments, not assumptions.* Never stop learning and discovering and re-understanding.
2. *No failure, only feedback.* Celebrate learning — whether it comes from success or failure.
3. *Iterate, don't procrastinate.* Set shorter time frames and smaller goals to build the muscle of high performance.

One way to frame strategy execution so that it makes room for learning is to think about it as a series of business experiments rather than as a fixed set of initiatives to be implemented on time and to budget. Our first mindset for inspiring *Learning* is therefore about using experiments so we never stop learning and discovering and re-understanding.

Experiments, not assumptions

Too many strategies are based on assumptions. Untested assumptions. And the problem with assumptions is that they're often wrong. How much money do you think your organisation spent last year on change or improvement that failed to produce what it was supposed to? And can you put your finger on the specific learning that any failures produced? These are uncomfortable questions, because we should have the answers, and usually don't. But evidence-based leaders can answer them, because they don't let assumptions run the show. Evidence-based leaders are scientists, but without the lab coat and pocket protector.

Experiments are what scientists use to stop assumptions from limiting how much they learn about the natural world. And we can use them in business to stop our assumptions from limiting how we can elevate performance, and from wasting the resources we invest to do it. Experiments need to be deliberately and carefully designed in order to convincingly and objectively do these things.

Well-chosen business experiments directly affect organisational performance, so they matter to us and our employees, our customers, our partners, our shareholders and our communities. We're always on a quest to improve the ROI of the organisation — to increase its performance for all its stakeholders, for the least effort and resources. So experimentation in business helps us test alternative change initiatives, so we can find out which will most likely have the biggest impact on organisational performance, and therefore are the best ones to invest in.

Web analytics uses experiments to improve website performance. Split tests, a very simple kind of experiment, are used all the time to test the impact of a design feature, such as colour, on how long people stay on a web page. Or to test the impact of different email subject lines on the rate at which people open the email to read it. These are very small tests, but they have quantifiable impacts on business success. If an email subject line gets a 10 per cent higher open rate, then that can translate into a 10 per cent increase in sales.

There are countless opportunities to use experiments in business, to find out what really works and what doesn't in closing performance gaps.

In business, our experiments don't need to have the same level of complexity or rigour that's required in drug testing or particle physics. But they do need to be well designed, and have enough rigour that we can be confident that they demonstrate what works and what doesn't.

Isolating the effect of a strategic initiative

People do naturally want to prove that their change initiatives worked. It helps them:

- celebrate success
- feel a sense of accomplishment
- boost their chances of winning more funding to continue their work.

And to prove the success of their initiatives, they know they must isolate the effect of those initiatives. But isolating the impact of a single initiative is impossible with so many confounding factors in such a complex system as an organisation. It's true that complexity gets in the way, but it only makes it impossible to isolate an initiative's impact *precisely*. We don't need to know the *precise* impact to decide if there was a *useful* impact. There are a few impact-isolating methods that can detect a useful impact.

Before, during, after

Time series analysis is the simplest but weakest form of isolating the impact of a change initiative on a targeted performance result, as other factors can also come into play over time. But if the odds of another factor having an impact at the exactly the same time are reasonably slim, it's still worth using this method to quantify the difference the change initiative has made.

We must, though, measure the performance result:

- before we execute the change
- regularly throughout the process of executing the change
- for some time after it's fully executed.

This way we'll have enough data to measure the difference, and correlate that difference to the time frame of the change. Displaying this data in an XmR chart (as discussed in chapter 7) is the perfect way to see if the differences are real. If we see a signal in the XmR chart that correlates with the point at which we expected to see the difference, and we can rule out other obvious factors, then it's looking like good news for the change initiative.

Control groups

Before we fully execute our change initiative, we can implement it on smaller scale for a portion — or sample — of our target population. We'd randomly divide the sample into two subgroups. One subgroup would be the control group, where we do not implement our change initiative. The other subgroup would be the treatment group, where we do execute our strategy.

For example, imagine our strategy is a new marketing campaign to encourage people to recycle more of their domestic rubbish. Our measure of the effect is the percentage of tonnes of domestic rubbish that is picked up by recycling rubbish trucks. We'd divide one of our rubbish collection zones into two groups, target the marketing campaign at just one of these groups, and track the measure for both groups separately. After the campaign, we'd look for a significant difference between the percentage of rubbish that went to recycling for the two groups.

Multivariate analysis

This simply means exploring the relationships between multiple variables or factors. In a quantitative sense, multivariate analysis means building a statistical model that numerically assesses the impact of several measures on a result. That usually needs the help of a statistician.

But we can also do it in a visual sense, using a collection of time-series graphs we can examine to find correlations and patterns among the measures. If we have a new strategy to increase sales revenue, such as a customer loyalty program that offers discounts for repeat purchases, how will we know it's working? Particularly if an economic downturn is affecting our industry, our marketing department is launching a new product, and we're concerned about several other factors that might confound the impact of our strategy. If we track and measure that range of factors each month, say — average industry sales, sales of new product, media mentions, and so on — then we can build a multivariate analysis using graphs that could highlight the impact of these factors on our outcome: sales revenue.

***

Even if these methods sound like a lot of effort, the truth of the matter is that, in relation to the effort we'll put into executing our strategies, they're a drop in the ocean. And if we don't use some method of isolating and testing the impact of our strategies, we're running the risk that our strategies could be a complete waste of time and money. It's lots of fun to prove that a change initiative is a success, but it's much harder to be open to the possibility

> We need to celebrate learning—whether it comes from success or failure.

that it failed. And we need to get this mindset about failure right, or we'll sabotage rather than inspire the organisational habit of *Learning*. We need to celebrate learning — whether it comes from success or failure.

No failure, only feedback

I have a message that I desperately want to share with the world, so reaching out to as many people as possible is critical to my success. One of my performance measures for tracking how well I reach out to people with the 'Prove it!' message is the number of weekly subscribers to my *Measure Up* newsletter, as shown in figure 10.1.

Figure 10.1: weekly subscriber numbers

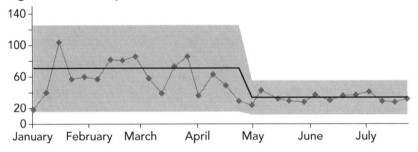

See the downward shift in May? Of course you can; it's huge. Something like that doesn't happen without an assignable cause. Figure 10.2 shows part of the story of what that cause actually is.

Figure 10.2: new subscribers

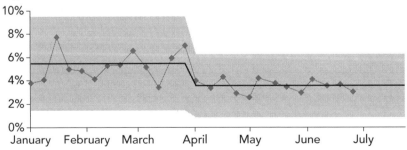

You can see a downward shift also happened in the percentage of new visitors who subscribe to *Measure Up*. It dropped from 5.4 per cent to 3.6 per cent almost overnight. *FAILURE!* One of my most important performance measures had taken a nose dive.

At that point I could have buried my head in the sand, and made up all kinds of rationalisations about why people aren't signing up for newsletters these days. Or blame myself for not being amazing enough. Or I could look deeper to find out what happened around that time that could have caused those sudden downward shifts. As it turned out, that was when I changed the way I invite people to sign up for *Measure Up*. I took away the free ebook I used to offer (it was called *202 Tips for Performance Measurement*), and in its place I offered a new free video course ('The 10 Secrets to KPI Success'). Developing the video course was supposed to increase sign-ups, but it did the exact opposite and significantly decreased them!

We don't like failure. On a personal level, it feels like *we* are the failure. We worry about looking stupid, losing face, damaging our reputation, and hampering our career prospects. And on a professional level, it weakens our position when we negotiate for future funding, and threatens the viability of our business unit or even the whole organisation. Our culture doesn't tolerate failure.

But as leaders, we have to be open about failure before we can expect that culture to change. When we can admit to failure, and celebrate the lessons we learn from it, it makes it easier for everyone else to do the same. Every failure we ignore is a missed lesson that could have been a boost in our pursuit of high performance.

We have to let failure change our mental models, so we can change our destiny; so we can change the thinking that created our performance problems in the first place. If we ignore failure, we ignore learning. Failure has to

> If we ignore failure, we ignore learning.

be framed as feedback. We should treat the advice of Adam Savage, of *Mythbusters*, as a mantra of evidence-based leadership:

> It's sort of a mental attitude about critical thinking and curiosity. It's about a mindset of looking at the world in a playful and curious and creative way.

Whether we're playful, curious and creative like Adam Savage, or whether we're stoic and matter-of-fact like his co-host Jamie Hyneman, it matters not. The point is that we're not judgemental about failure.

The right kind of failure

The kind of failure we can most easily be comfortable with is the failure we design to have, so that we can get feedback we can learn from. High-performance organisations are deliberate about the change initiatives they implement and, when change initiatives begin with business experiments that inform their ultimate implementation, we are designing the right kind of failures to have. They are failures that tell us quickly and inexpensively what we shouldn't do.

The right kind of failure is simply feedback from our experiments that teaches us what doesn't work. Thomas Edison famously said something like, 'I have not failed. I've just found 10 000 ways that won't work.' He had thousands of failures that quickly and inexpensively told him how not to create a light bulb. We don't have to steel ourselves to cope with thousands of failures, and we can often avoid many by learning from the failures of others who have gone before us. This is one of the powerful uses of benchmarking: discovering the ways that great organisations do what we're trying to do better. We need to design failures that build upon knowledge like that, not reinvent it. Or worse, blindly repeat the same mistakes of the past, learning nothing. For example:

- A printer manufacturer built on the knowledge of a knitwear company, which dyed sweaters after they were knitted, to avoid a high inventory of printers that didn't match fast-changing customer preferences.
- A rifle company built on a cosmetics company's lipstick case technology to make their bullet casings shinier.

- An eye hospital in India built on a hamburger chain's social media strategies to use social media to get their messages out to the masses.

The right kind of failure is when we're testing something that hasn't already been tested, and we find out it doesn't work. When failure creates new knowledge, it's worth it. When it just repeats the mistakes of the past, it's wasteful. So the hypotheses for our business experiments shouldn't come from a brainstorming session or

> When failure creates new knowledge, it's worth it.

even from the 'wisdom' of a single executive. We should do our best to base our hypotheses on plausible ideas that haven't been tested in relation to closing our performance gaps. This means we need to do our due diligence before we decide what change initiatives to test; we need to go find out what has already failed in the past, and avoid repeating the mistake.

Breaking the framework of failure

Systems thinking is a not a new concept, but to many people in today's business world it is. So it's no surprise that thinking systemically when using performance measures to improve performance doesn't come naturally. Systems thinking gives us a framework to find clues about what's at the root of performance problems, and what to do about it. Systems thinking is considering the:

- whole
- big picture
- elements that make the whole
- interaction of these elements with each other.

It means thinking about relationships in a dynamic way, as opposed to a static way, like a movie as opposed to a photograph. Understanding these dynamics speeds up our learning about which changes will get the results we want.

There are several common dynamics — or system archetypes — in business systems, and Peter Senge details them in his book *The Fifth*

Discipline. There are two types of system archetypes: reinforcing and balancing.

Reinforcing

Reinforcing archetypes describe the dynamic at the root of a performance result that is growing. For example, when employee engagement deepens, it creates better conditions for organisational performance to improve, which then intrinsically rewards employees, and their engagement deepens even further. Reinforcing archetypes can also describe the dynamic at the root of a performance result that is declining.

Balancing

Balancing archetypes describe the dynamic that's causing a performance result to stagnate, and resist change. When there is an explicit target or goal, or an implicit one, a balancing system self-corrects to maintain the target or goal. Perhaps we want to decrease rework, but it refuses to budge, even though we're educating people about how to avoid rework, and we're offering incentives to reduce it. Rework isn't reducing because something else is holding it in place. We need to look for the balancing dynamic, to find the self-correcting behaviour that's holding rework in place. It might be that when staff take the time to reduce rework, the pressure of hitting deadlines increases, and so they have to work harder and faster again to catch up, and rework increases again.

***

The thing about system dynamics is that there is no use finding someone or something to blame. The dynamic is held in place by the interrelationships among the parts of the system.

Comparing performance to others might momentarily inspire people to aim higher, but it won't change the system. Setting expectations of where performance should be, with quotas or targets to hit, might get everyone trying harder for a while, but it won't change the

> Comparison and expectation provide a framework for failure.

system. And it will feel like failure. Comparison and expectation provide a framework for failure. We have to break that framework. Feedback about what the system is actually doing is all that matters.

The most useful feedback comes from business experiments at the system level, to find out how a specific change affects the system's dynamic, and learn from whether it worked or not. We need to be prepared to look honestly at how things currently are. We can't be afraid to see that past solutions, even those we instigated or supported, have failed, even if it's taken us a long time to notice. From now on, we want to design failures that give us powerful feedback to speed up our learning.

Equally importantly, systems thinking helps us disassociate ourselves (our egos) from what the system is doing. With the stoic curiosity of a scientist and the creative playfulness of a child, we can forget about comparison and expectation (the framework that makes space for failure), and simply learn.

Aim high, but without expectation

Stretch targets are scary because they can feel impossible. Most of the time people will avoid them or ignore them, for fear of failing to meet them. What they don't realise is that they are guaranteeing a fate worse than failure.

It's natural to feel uneasy and apprehensive about something we don't know how to achieve yet. That's the nature of big targets: they are heights that we can't reach with what we already know and do. Without question, we have to move outside of our comfort zone when we pursue big targets — and outside of our comfort zone is where we feel fear. Not of death or injury of course, but of failure.

For some, the failure of falling short of a big target brings:

- embarrassment
- frustration
- loss of face
- loss of respect
- disappointment
- reinforcement of an already low self-esteem.

We take refuge behind 'achievable targets', blind to the truth about big targets.

What really happens when we fail to achieve a big target is this: we end up achieving far more than we would otherwise have achieved if we'd chosen a safe and achievable target. Safe and achievable targets don't:

- stretch us
- ask us to become more than we currently are
- ask us to think smarter, or choose more wisely or act more deliberately
- ask us to question our approaches, look beyond our current knowledge or challenge our assumptions.

The most that an achievable target can get us to do is to work harder. That's not what high-performance organisations do.

We need to shift ourselves before we can shift our performance. Stretch targets demand that we simultaneously think about the result we're aiming for *and* the adventure of getting there. Simultaneously we must be results-oriented and present in the moment, aligning our thoughts and choices and actions in the here and now with that tantalising destination in the future. We can't get caught up measuring how far we fall short of a big target. We must measure how far it pulled us forward. And then we start another iteration of reaching for that big target.

> Stretch targets demand that we simultaneously think about the result we're aiming for *and* the adventure of getting there.

Iterating our way to success, rather than leaping to success, is another important mindset for inspiring the evidence-based leadership practice of *Learning*. It's about setting shorter time frames and smaller goals to build the muscle of high performance.

Iterate, don't procrastinate

Failure isn't something we want to focus too much of our time on, obviously. Ultimately, we want success to be centre stage. We want to be fast to fail, so we can be fast to learn, and reach success sooner. Success loves speed.

But we don't want to trade rigour for speed, either. We need a practical way to have the right kind of failure, and waste no time in arriving at success. And this practical way requires us to approach problem solving quite a bit differently to what we're familiar with.

The following is an explanation organisational behaviour expert Margaret J. Wheatley, in her book *Leadership and the New Science*, gives us of why we don't get much success by studying problems in detailed isolation and implementing their solutions as big bangs. As you read it, remember learning to play a musical instrument, ride a bike or play soccer:

> We expand our vision to see the whole, then narrow our gaze to peer intently into the individual moments. With each iteration, we see more of the whole, and gain new understandings about the individual elements. We paint a portrait of the whole, surfacing as much detail as possible. Then we inquire into a few pivotal events or decisions, and search for great detail there also. We keep dancing between the two levels … If we hold awareness of the whole as we study the part, and understand the part in its relationship to the whole, profound new insights become available.

We cannot master music, sport, art or any other worthwhile endeavour by studying the theory alone, or by practising just one piece of it. We can't master it in one fell swoop, no matter how big that swoop is. We need to follow ever-expanding cycles of think and do. We need to iterate, and let each iteration inform the next.

The foundation of each iteration is the plan–do–study–act (PDSA) cycle, one of W. Edwards Deming's gifts to the world and the heart of just about every performance improvement method that has stood the test of time since. It means that we deliberately plan a change initiative. Then we implement it. We study what happened, using performance measures and other data, to see if it worked or not, and learn from it. Then we act on what we've learned from the data. It might then mean another iteration is required, to build on what we've learned, or to close a bit more of the performance gap. A business experiment is a single PDSA cycle. The execution of a strategy is usually a series of PDSA cycles.

It's vitally important to maintain momentum as we iterate our way through the execution of our strategy, for three good reasons:

1. If we keep the pace up, we keep the energy high and people will have a better experience than if we draw it out too long.

2. If we fail fast we can learn sooner, so we only ever need to make small course corrections (which are much less costly than big corrections).

3. By moving quickly we can chip away at our performance gaps as we go, get some quick wins, and get a return on our investment sooner too.

Fast and focused iterations

Instead of implementing our change initiatives as long, drawn-out projects, we can run them as a series of iterations. There's a clear parallel to Google Venture's design sprints, explored in chapter 9. And to business experiments, discussed earlier in this chapter. In the context of evidence-based leadership, a single series of iterations could be focused specifically on closing one performance gap: one specific performance measure of one specific goal.

But just as validly, a single series of iterations might focus specifically on one strategic or operational goal, and each iteration might focus on a different performance measure. The goal might be to reduce workplace accidents. The first iteration might focus on increasing the reporting of near misses, and the simple raising of awareness could be enough to see a small reduction in workplace accidents. The second iteration might focus on the most prevalent near miss, such as trips and falls, and, by making it easier to keep workplaces uncluttered, it could take another chip out of the workplace accident performance gap. And so on.

The iteration cycle

Inspired by Josh Kaufman's WIGWAM model, from his book *The Personal MBA*, there are six steps in the iteration cycle.

1. Now

The first step is to assess how things are right now. Our performance measure will tell us what's happening. Specifically, it will tell us how big the gap between actual performance and our target is. If this isn't our first iteration in attempting to close this particular performance gap, then we also want to notice whether the last iteration worked or not, and take that knowledge into the next step of the iteration cycle.

2. Options

The second step in the iteration cycle is when we build on previous learning, both our own and others', to scope the options for change. We take a closer look at:

- the business process flow
- what system dynamic might be at play
- the root causes, using whatever data we have to help us quantify each of their impacts on the performance gap
- whether others have already tackled a similar problem, by benchmarking, for example, and list the solutions that failed and the solutions that worked.

3. Focus

The third step in the iteration cycle is to choose just one cause to fix, the one that the data suggests will take the biggest bite out of the current performance gap, and is within our circle of influence. It will be tempting to fix a few things; it will feel more efficient. But it means we confound our learning. We won't be able to isolate the impact of each change, and so we won't know which changes worked, which changes did nothing, and which changes actually made things worse. If we treat this as a business experiment, it's here that we form our testable hypothesis.

4. Approach

The fourth step in the iteration cycle is to design how the chosen cause will be fixed. It's designing the change initiative that we believe will close up the performance gap, at least a bit. If we're treating it as a business experiment, this will include designing a control group or data for a baseline, and selecting a representative sample to test the change initiative.

5. Implement

We simply carry out the action plan, and collect data to measure the impact of the change initiative and any unintended consequences of it.

6. Learn

The sixth and final step of the iteration cycle is checking the performance gap again, using the measure of the result we used in the first step. We want to learn what impact our change initiative had on the performance gap. If we use an XmR chart for our performance measure, then one way to see the impact will be a signal in the chart, such as a long run or a short run. And the impact of the change initiative will be the difference between the new level of performance (the central line) and the previous one. We also want to learn about any unintended consequences, too, to be sure the impact of the change is worth the true cost. And now, if we want to close even more of the performance gap, or set a higher target to create a new gap, we move back around the cycle to the first step again.

*****

Iterating our way toward a closed performance gap is going to be faster than trying to close that gap with a single big solution. It's different to putting all our eggs into one basket — planning and budgeting for the entire year's change initiatives at the start — and hoping it all pays off in the end. It's less risky and often less costly too. That makes for a higher return on investment in our strategy, and higher organisational performance. And it will help us nip procrastination in the bud.

One reason you might procrastinate in mastering evidence-based leadership, and leading your organisation to high-performance, is overwhelm. So much to do, so little time. All these evidence-based leadership habits and mindsets sound well and good — but you'll get to it when you have the time.

The truth — and you know it — is that you don't have the time now because there isn't enough evidence-based leadership going on. It's a vicious cycle: the more you wait, the more you need it. So how can you start, now?

ITERATE, DON'T PROCRASTINATE

Iterating our way toward a closed performance gap is going to be faster than trying to close that gap with a single big solution. It's less risky and often less costly too. That makes for a higher ROI in our strategy, and higher organisational performance.

CHAPTER 11

START NOW: EVIDENCE-BASED LEADERSHIP STARTS AT THE TOP

Measurement is the most practical way to start the journey to a high-performance organisation. Measuring what matters (and doing it properly, as early chapters discuss) shifts the way people think about:

- performance
- their contribution to the organisation
- why they come to work each day.

I see it happen all the time. Executive teams routinely say to me that the conversation to re-articulate their direction in measurable terms is one of the best conversations they've had — a conversation they should have had years ago. Operational staff say they feel excited about their new measures, and that for the first time they can see a bigger reason for coming to work — bigger than their job and bigger than themselves. Start the journey to high performance with measurement, because it's really not about the numbers. It's about the way we see and appreciate and connect ourselves with what high performance is all about.

Dean Spitzer talks about organisational performance like no-one else I know. His book, *Transforming Performance Measurement*, is a classic. My copy has highlighter on every other page, but one of the most powerful things he has to say is this:

> The key to success is MEASUREMENT. Measurement done right can transform your organization... measurement is fundamental to high performance, improvement, and, ultimately, success in business, or in any other area of human endeavor.

Know that you only need to decide to take the first step on this path. Then momentum and small wins can build on each other, like a reinforcing loop, and the subsequent steps, one at a time, will be so much easier to continue with.

A high-performance culture is an output, not an input

In their article in *HBR*'s April 2016 issue, 'Culture Is Not the Culprit', Jay W. Lorsch and Emily McTague rightly point out that fixing the culture is rarely the right solution to organisational performance problems. Rather, they describe how great leaders don't wait for a performance culture to enable measurement; they use measurement to enable a performance culture. Culture is an outcome of, not an input to, organisational performance.

> Culture is an outcome of, not an input to, organisational performance.

And the way that performance measurement and improvement is practised will have a direct impact on the culture that emerges. What we do is what we become.

John Kotter really understands culture and how to lead change. In his article 'The Key to Changing Organizational Culture' in *Forbes*, he confirms that culture doesn't change by edict. Culture can only change slowly, and when it's led by someone at the top, or by a group that's big enough and influential enough. And what they do to lead a culture change is practise the new behaviours themselves. They spotlight the better results that come from those new behaviours. And in time, in an organic way, the culture turns.

Woven throughout this book is the message that when measures are used to monitor people's performance and reward or punish them, a defensive culture will emerge. People will not embrace accountability for performance. They will fear bad results and blame, and consequently will either hide them, or turn attention to good news only. Trust, openness, and collaboration will deteriorate, and performance won't improve.

The central theme of this book, however, is that when performance measures are used to monitor results and diagnose how to elevate performance, a different culture emerges. People will embrace accountability as the practice of problem solving, not blame. They will be curious and collaborative, and consequently will appreciate how to work *on* the business and not just *in* it. Ownership and transparency will increase, and performance will improve.

The easiest way to commit to evidence-based leadership, and immediately start turning around the culture and facing it toward high performance, is to measure, and measure for the right reasons. John Kotter predicted this, back in 1996 when he wrote the first edition of *Leading Change*:

> Keeping urgency up will require, first and foremost, performance information systems that are far superior to what we generally see today...The systems that supply this information cannot be designed, as are some today, to make the organization or one of its units look good. They will need to be created to provide honest and unvarnished news, especially about performance.

This means we must:

- measure the results that matter
- measure them meaningfully and honestly and openly
- engage people in creating and using those measures
- focus on process improvement as the underlying approach to strategy execution.

And the fastest way to commit to evidence-based leadership is to start from the top: the senior leadership team.

The first iteration of evidence-based leadership

Starting at the top means that the senior leadership team, led by the CEO, begins practising the habits of evidence-based leadership before asking anything of the rest of the organisation. They will be practising

the habits of *Direction* and *Evidence* and *Execution*. Starting at the top is the quickest and easiest way to get rolling on the journey of high performance, because employees follow what leaders do. It's too risky for them to do otherwise. Even if

The implementation of evidence-based practice organisation-wide will follow iterations.

leaders say with great gusto 'Start measuring what matters!', nothing will change if they aren't doing it themselves.

The implementation of evidence-based practice organisation-wide will follow iterations. It will never happen if we wait to thoroughly research our current state, meticulously devise a change management plan, garner enough budget to resource it all, and schedule the implementation for when the time is just right and the planets have lined up. We don't wait until:

- we have great business intelligence systems
- the next planning cycle starts
- the dust from the reorganisation has settled.

We need evidence-based management to make all this, and just about everything else, work.

There are five stages in the first iteration of implementing evidence-based management across the organisation.

- *Stage 1:* The senior leadership team decides to pursue evidence-based leadership.
- *Stage 2:* The habits of *Direction* and *Evidence* are applied, to test and improve the measurability of the strategic direction, and develop the measures that will prove it.

- *Stage 3:* The strategy is communicated, in a very engaging way, to inspire *Decision* across the organisation. This will kick-start the cascading of the strategy down into the processes of the organisation, using a performance measurement approach, such as PuMP.
- *Stage 4:* As the performance measurement approach is implemented, it naturally inspires *Action*, the closing of performance gaps in alignment with the strategic direction. While the strategy is cascaded, the senior leadership team continues with the habit of *Execution*, to create and use their strategic performance measures to lead the execution of strategy.
- *Stage 5: Learning* is inspired, to reflect on how performance was influenced throughout the first iteration, and prepare for the next cycle of strategic planning, which will kick off the next iteration of evidence-based management.

Stage 1: Decide to be evidence-based leaders

Perhaps you already are an evidence-based leader. But how can you know if that's true, or just a perception?

- How well have the habits and processes of evidence-based leadership, outlined in this book, been embedded in your everyday practice as a leader, and the practices of people throughout the organisation?
- Are you already quantifying the return on investment that your organisation generates?
- Can you prove, objectively and convincingly, that the organisation is:
  — fulfilling its mission
  — delivering on its purpose
  — making its vision a reality?

Answering these questions easily is a good indicator that you're already an evidence-based leader. But, from my experience, at least, the vast majority of organisations cannot answer these questions easily, or at all.

It's worth having the conversation with your leadership team. It's worth exploring the leadership habits of *Direction*, *Evidence* and *Execution*, and the organisational habits of *Decision*, *Action* and *Learning*. What do they mean to you? How do you see them practised? Where is there the opportunity to master them?

And this is a conversation for the whole leadership team, not just part of it. The CEO of a sporting association invited me to facilitate a workshop where he and his executive team would develop measures for their strategic goals. But the CEO didn't attend the first day of the workshop, where we focused on how to make goals measurable by removing the weasel words. Despite his belief in measurement and his enthusiasm for his executives to buy in to their new measures, his involvement on the second day was disruptive. He wanted to return to the weasel words, and his executives now knew why they shouldn't. Because the CEO wasn't involved from the start, too much time was wasted and the buy-in was hampered. This first conversation, about what evidence-based leadership is all about, and how it is implemented, is too important for any member of the senior leadership team to miss.

Stage 2: Create a measurable corporate strategy

The first active step of evidence-based leadership is to make your corporate strategy:

- more measurable
- easier to communicate
- directly monitored with meaningful measures.

Because so many strategic goals are written in intangible, weasely language, we start with testing how measurable the current goals really are. Goals need to be written as results (not actions) and with words that a 10-year-old could comprehend. The goals should be reworded so their true meaning is much more apparent to everyone. This automatically makes them easier to measure.

Then we build quantitative measures from the evidence that most convinces us of each goal being achieved, and is feasible to gather. The collection of reworded goals and their measures are mapped visually, to bring them together into a story of the corporate strategy, highlighting the relationships that connect each part. In PuMP this is called a Results Map (as discussed in chapter 8), and it's the foundation for easily communicating and cascading the strategy throughout the organisation. It helps to build a line of sight for each team, from the results they will focus on all the way through to their ultimate impact on the strategic goals.

During one of these 'strategic KPI' workshops for the timber company discussed in chapter 3, the CEO remarked that, with their new Results Map, he had multiplied himself by 12 — because now his entire leadership team could tell the same story about the company's strategy.

Stage 3: Cascade the strategy

Emailing the strategic plan to everyone, with a cover letter by the CEO, isn't going to get the level of buy-in that's necessary to fully execute it. People need to be engaged in a discussion about the strategic plan, they need to ponder it, to ask questions, to challenge it. Then they can make it their own.

We need to create space for people to ponder the strategic plan, to ask questions of it, and to hypothesise what their team's contribution to it is. Owen Harrison, in his book *Open Space Technology*, sets just one law that makes open and collaborative spaces work: the law of two feet. It means than each person is responsible for choosing how, where, when and if they contribute. This law allows buy-in to happen naturally, because free choice is fundamental to it. Using this law of two feet in communicating strategy creates communication that is:

- two-way, like a dialogue
- unstructured, to allow for exploration
- flexible, so people can join in on their own terms.

Their buy-in to the strategy begins here. And we can't miss this first opportunity to inspire the organisational habit of *Decision*.

This step is a great way to kick-start the cascading of strategy. But before that begins, we've found it very useful to form a core group of people who can be the champions and facilitators of the cascading, and give them the skill and knowledge to do it in an evidence-based way. PuMP is our methodology of choice, and so these champions and facilitators are trained in this method so they're ready to lead their teams through the organisational habits of *Decision*, *Action* and *Learning*.

Stage 4: Let the cascade flow naturally

One mistake organisations make in performance measurement is to not have a real method. They treat measuring performance as an ad hoc activity or event. But when we adopt a performance measurement method such as PuMP, another mistake is to do too much too soon. Starting small with this stage is important for a few reasons. We can overwhelm people with too much change, and burn them out. They'll make mistakes without noticing, and leave them uncorrected. They'll feel out of their depth and lack confidence when they need it most. They'll fail to get a measurable return on investment, which is so important in maintaining their momentum to continue when it gets tough.

So we start cascading strategy in small bites, with teams pilot-testing the measurement method before they implement it fully. They will form Measures Teams, and be led by one of the champions or facilitators we trained in Stage 3. They will focus on just one goal that describes their contribution to the organisation's strategic direction. They will measure that one goal. They will use the measure to guide them in improving performance and closing the performance gap that will make the goal reality. What they are doing is working through the organisational habits of *Decision*, *Action* and *Learning*.

As leaders, our job is to show up with inspiration as the teams move through these processes.

Starting small in this first iteration has some very worthwhile advantages. First, they get some time to learn and master it first, before the pressure is on to measure and improve everything that matters. We have to implement and practise, fail and learn, before we've earned our stripes.

Second, before people are really sold on a new idea, they need proof it works. And that means they need to see an early ROI.

Third, a measurement pilot makes it easier to notice and handle setbacks. When we give people the opportunity to learn in a low-pressure environment there is less consequence if they fail (and they will fail). They need this time to reframe failure as learning, if that's not already ingrained in the culture.

Fourth, a pilot approach makes it easier for people to participate, over and above their 'real work'. The low cost of participation means that more people will experience the power of measuring what matters, and quickly come to see that measurement *is* a part of 'real work'. And then real engagement builds naturally.

Many of the stories I've shared in this book are from pilot PuMP implementations that people have shared with me over the years. They started small, and the interest of other teams grew organically. Ultimately, measurement is everybody's job. Everyone in the organisation has some responsibility for what they create, both deliberately and unintentionally, as they carry out their job tasks. So we let the

> Let the practice of measuring what matters soak across the entire organisation, without force.

practice of measuring what matters soak across the entire organisation, without force. Wherever there is energy to learn and improve from measuring, we let it happen.

Stage 5: Reflect and learn for the next iteration

Did we close our performance gaps? What was the return on the investment in doing that? What did we learn about the dynamics driving performance in our processes and systems? What did we learn from attempts to close the performance gaps that didn't work? What did we learn about ourselves? What is the next most important thing to focus on, to close our performance gaps further?

These are the questions we ask ourselves at this point. We will tweak our approach. We will reinforce it with another iteration. And we will celebrate what we've accomplished: both the learning and the improved performance.

A great thing about deliberately reflecting on questions like these is that the answers become part of the analysis that precedes strategy formulation. We understand the organisation better, the processes and system dynamics and root causes that constrain its performance. We understand our performance strengths, and our next performance improvement opportunities. This is a good part of what the next strategic plan should focus on. And that will kick off the next iteration of practising evidence-based leadership.

Will you start?

Mastery of something as complex as leading an organisation to high performance doesn't happen quickly. It's hard, it's challenging, and it's a long road. But we need you on that road. You're not just leading a bunch of people to get stuff done. You're leading our quality of life. Don't organisations exist to make life better for people? For shareholders, customers, partners, employees and the community? All those people invest something in your organisation: their time, their money, their energy, their thoughts and ideas — even some of their autonomy and freedom. And don't they deserve a return on that investment?

You, as a leader, hold the space for high performance to happen. When you start, they will follow.

APPENDIX: XMR CHARTS GIVE US THREE SIGNALS

XmR charts monitor the outputs of processes to provide a rapid and reliable means of detecting change in those outputs. Walter A. Shewhart was the statistician who invented this style of chart, back in 1924. He used them to monitor the production quality of underground transmission equipment at the Western Electric Company. Since then, these charts have rocked the world.

What many managers today still don't realise is that Shewhart's approach to analysing data for manufacturing performance is just as applicable and transformational for non-manufacturing performance results. We can use Shewhart's charts to monitor:

- profit
- revenue
- expenses
- staff turnover
- on-time delivery

- budget variation
- customer satisfaction
- employee engagement
- sales
- lost time injuries.

Dr Donald Wheeler, a renowned statistician of our time, wrote *Understanding Variation: The Key to Managing Chaos* on this very topic. Wheeler introduced the use of the XmR chart for management data, or, as we call it, performance measurement. His closing remarks in this best-selling management book are worth repeating here:

> Millions of people have proven, by their own experiences, over the past 60 years, that Shewhart's control charts work. This approach to understanding and using data is not on trial. The question is not whether or not the techniques will work—but rather whether or not you will make them work.

The power of XmR charts is how clearly and accurately they show us signals of change, despite the natural variability that every measure has. Here are the three most common signals.

Signal 1: Outlier or special cause

When a measure value falls outside the natural process limits, it means that more than just the routine variation is at play. It's a signal that something else has happened. If employee attendance suddenly plummets below the bottom natural process limit, a likely cause could be a flu epidemic or local natural disaster that kept many more people away from work. Even though this is a signal that something out of the ordinary has happened, because it's just a one-time event, we don't react to it. We find out what caused it, but we don't run around madly trying to fix it. That would be a massive waste of time and money because we'd essentially be trying to fix something that won't happen again, or that is completely outside our control. An outlier is illustrated in figure A.1.

Figure A.1: an outlier

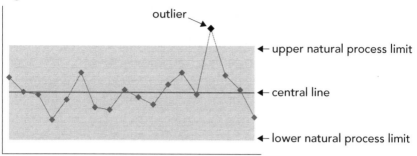

Signal 2: Long run

To be convinced that a change in the level of performance has happened, we need to see eight (yes, eight) points in a row on the same side of the central line. The probability that a pattern such as that is part of routine variation is close to zero (0.78%, to be precise).

If a measure of invoice accuracy showed a long run above the central line, it might be evidence that an initiative to simplify the pricing strategy successfully reduced the errors in invoices. When we see a long run signal in our measure, we certainly need to find the cause for it. Sometimes it will be a signal of improvement, and we want to confirm what caused the improvement. Other times it will be a signal that performance has deteriorated and the cause of that is very important to identify! A long run is illustrated in figure A.2.

Figure A.2: a long run

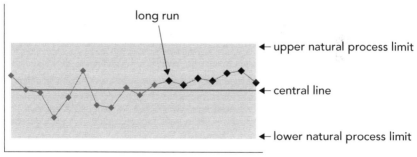

Signal 3: Short run

You're no doubt thinking to yourself, 'I can't wait for eight months before I can know if I should take action!' We can either measure more frequently to pick up signals sooner (if it makes sense to), or plan for bigger signals. A bigger signal appears as a short run, of three out of four consecutive measure values closer to a natural process limit than they are to the central line. The probability of this pattern happening within routine variation also has a very close to zero probability.

A short run above the central line for on-time deliveries for a trucking company would likely be due to an initiative that had a substantially large impact. It could be something like doubling the fleet size. But it also could be a new competitor in the market that poached a large percentage of their customers. Again, with a signal like the short run, it's really important to find the cause before responding. A short run is illustrated in figure A.3.

Figure A.3: a short run

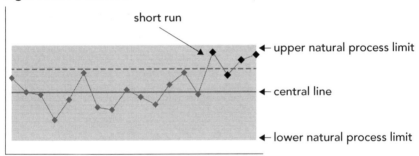

INDEX

innovation 49, 62–63, 107, 112
iteration 169–173, 178

jargon 28, 40–44, 58, 62, 110, 112,
    180
Jones, Daniel T. 145
judgement, of employees 28,
    53–61, 96–97, 119, 121, 177

Kaplan, Robert Steven 7, 11
Kaufman, Josh 171–173
key performance indicators
    (KPIs) 53–55, 75, 88–89, 106,
    107–108, 147
Knapp, Jake 142
Kotter, John 176–177
Kowitz, Braden 142

leaders *see also* CEOs
    — habits for 33–102
    — responsibilities of 24, 34
leadership *see also* evidence-based
    leadership
    — style of 3, 7, 12, 21–22
    — successful 9, 12
Lean Six Sigma 95, 144–145, 148
Lean Thinking method 144–145
learning 79, 183–184
Learning (organisational habit)
    26, 27, 28–29, 155–173
leverage 27, 28, 36, 79–82, 84, 86,
    90, 93, 94, 109, 118, 122, 124,
    130, 137–138
Lorsch, Jay W. 176

marketing 10, 86, 91, 109, 116,
    118, 136, 160–161
Mason, Jim 11–12
McChesney, Chris 44, 106
McTague, Emily 176

Meadows, Donella 155
measurement *see* impact,
    measuring; performance,
    measuring
Measures Gallery 106
Microsoft 4
mindset 7, 26, 27–30, 39, 43, 79,
    86–87, 158, 199
mission, organisational 3–8, 28,
    53, 112
    — CEO's role in 7, 15
    — clarity of 5–7, 12
    — measuring 7
    — statement of 3, 4
models for measurement 9, 48–49
motivating employees 38, 58, 122,
    130
multivariate analysis 161

nonprofit organisations 4–5
Norton, David P. 11

O'Neill, Paul 52
objectives 9, 25–26, 30, 44–45,
    50, 52, 53, 61–62, 105–126
organisational habits 103–184
ownership 7, 23, 26, 29, 49,
    104–125, 177

Pareto chart 139–140
Pareto, Vilfredo 137
Parmenter, David 53
PATH 4–5
patterns, in data 13, 27, 82–93
    — seeing big picture 84–85
    — variability 83–84
people vs. processes 94–100
perfectionism, avoiding 29,
    137–149
performance dashboards 87–88

Did this book help you? I'd love to know.

And I'd love to hear about your own experiences with leading a high-performance culture, with handling the tension between transparency and accountability, and with measuring your organisation's success. Let me know via **proveit@staceybarr.com**.

I'm writing on new thoughts about measurement and evidence-based leadership just about every week, and you can make sure you get the lastest ideas by joining thousands of other subscribers to my newsletter, *Measure Up*, at **www.staceybarr.com/signup**.

If you'd like help with creating and growing your high-performance culture and mastering evidence-based leadership, you can find out more at **www.staceybarr.com**.

Photo by Laura Maxwell and Melissa Kneipp

Made in the USA
Middletown, DE
11 April 2017